WORDPRESS FOR BEGINNERS

HOW TO USE WORDPRESS!

MICHAEL MCGINNIS

TABLE OF CONTENTS

INTRODUCTION

This book is deemed useful for any individual who has ever longed for a simple, yet effective approach to design and create a website or any form of online presence and wasn't certain of how to begin. Through this book, we have focused on helping a huge number of individuals begin utilizing wordpress and learning web plan. Therefore, before you begin, be sure that wordpress is the answer to your web needs and leave the rest to us. By the end of this book, you are sure to possess all the information you require to get started on wordpress.

Wordpress? What is it?

Wordpress is an open source blogging package. In fact, the unique selling point of this framework is its ability to manage content and work well as a content management framework, a general website and a website programming framework. This makes it simple for anybody to set up, oversee and keep up a site without having a formal degree or expertise in the field.

The wordpress story began in 2003 when it was first introduced. Today, it has grown to become the biggest platform in the blogging world. The growing popularity of this platform is far reaching and wordpress has earned a great reputation and user base.

For instance, the New York Times runs its websites utilizing wordpress. That ought to let you know about the level of functionality and security of the information wordpress is capable of offering. However, don't be bogged down by a complicated terminology. Wordpress is also utilized by many other individuals and organizations who have never touched any sort of web configuration framework before. So it is easy to use for even clients with non-technical backgrounds.

Before anything else, it is worth a mention that wordpress is an open source platform and is available to one and all free of cost. However, unlike the common perception, anything that comes free is not usable. However, it does not make wordpress incapable or inefficient in any respect. In fact, its free accessibility allows users and designers from all over the world to improve, enhance and better it. The rich online community that backs wordpress development is its biggest strength.

Wordpress, the platform, allows the user to create content in two formats – pages and posts. These two content components make up your website's content. The fundamental difference between these two categories of content that wordpress acknowledges is the latter is time driven while the former is static.

In addition, it is possible to deal with your site's look and feel with subjects. These are handcrafts that allows you to control the elements of your website and how the same is sorted out. In case, you're acquainted with the expression "format" simply substitutes the expression "subject" when discussing Wordpress. The product is very adjustable, and has truly large number of "plugin" bits of programming so almost everything on your website can be put into place. Plugins are the soul of wordpress and we shall discuss them in greater detail as we move along.

Wordpress can deal with a few sorts of content for you, including links, pages and posts. Considering the fact wordpress was created with the objective to make blogging easier, posts are your essential content, which is saved on the basis of the timestamp of posting and are utilized for standard website sections. You may compose posts month to month, week after week, every day or several times a day. Everything relies on upon the motivation behind the creation of your website and its purpose.

Pages are essentially posts that are not sorted on the basis of the time they were published. The foundation of your website is this content and the pages hence created add to the website menu. They are fundamentally the same as any static page on a customary website. However, it surely is a ton simpler to make and without needing to pay somebody else to accomplish the task for you. Lastly, links are just what they seem to be – links. You can utilize interfaces all through your pages and posts, and additionally in your sidebar. This can be helpful for a rundown of suggested administrations or supportive destinations.

Section or functional boxes on a website are called widgets. They are simply helpful dandy boxes you frequently encounter if you look at either half of the website. They don't need to be placed at a specific position. You can place them at any location you desire. However, with that said, it is obvious why individuals consider to them. You can add infinite functional levels to your website, some of which include a membership box, supplement pictures and features, put extraordinary calls-to-activity, list your latest posts, include simple routes along any of the sides of the page, or pretty much any other possibilities you need.

Is Wordpress For You?

Now that you know what wordpress is, an obvious question that may arise in your mind is: who can utilize wordpress? Anybody is the simple yet most appropriate answer to this question. Wordpress is a really capable framework and it can undoubtedly be tweaked for your needs. There are subjects particularly intended for numerous types of situations, including websites, scaled down locales, online stores, online magazines, photographic exhibitions and that's just the beginning.

A Wordpress site can function admirably for pretty much anybody. Some of the common purposes for which wordpress is commonly used include:

- Service-arranged organizations like land operators, auto merchants, and so on
- Small organizations and huge corporations
- Food providers, restaurants and designers
- Specialists and consultants
- Schools, churches and charities
- Craftsmen, bands and professionals belonging to the creative field.
- Professionals searching for a job

- Families making a family history to impart
- Scrapbook fans.
- Individuals pursuing their hobbies in the form of websites.

Genuinely, Wordpress is a platform that anyone can use and benefit from.

Can you Benefit From Wordpress?

Next up, how can wordpress benefit you? Here are the five main advantages that wordpress is known to offer to its clients and users.

- The product is free!
  How often have you got something free that is completely utilitarian and prepared to utilize? Moreover, if you wish to upgrade your website using premium themes and plugins, despite everything you're going to shell out huge amounts of cash over the amount you are most likely to spend a handcrafted website.
- Extremely easy to use and learn
  Truly. If you know how to use a computer and you are capable of doing simple tasks like sending an email or operating a facebook account, wordpress should come easy to you. Moreover, if you have a working knowledge of how the Internet works and what you need to open and use a website, you should not face any major problems while working with wordpress. With wordpress, you can include and erase pages, posts, sidebar components, and others without unintentionally derailing the general configuration of your site. So, the risk of making a mistake is rather low.
- User possesses all the control
  Possessing ownership of your website, and having the capacity to roll out improvements of the same without the intervention of an expert, is a definitive advantage in online flexibility. You don't need to depend on a high-demanding website developer, architect or designer to roll out improvements or fix issues that may arise on your website at whatever

point they can pressurize you. You're in total control of what is going on with your website and how much you are spending on the same.

- Web Crawler Advantages

   Web crawlers adore destinations that are not difficult to index. Wordpress gives them a very favorable arrangement to work with in addition to regularly updated content. That is the place blogging comes into play so pleasantly. Just by maintaining your business or individual site and speaking with your users in a manner that keeps them regularly to you, you'll be creating crisp, substantial content the Internet searchers can hardly wait to get tightly adhered to.

- A Huge Support Community

   Wordpress isn't simply a product; it has turned into a group. Some may even say a development forum. Truth be told, Wordcamps or 1-3 days preparing sessions have been arranged by several corporate endeavors. They are casual, group launched and group composed of events set up, by different wordpress users, who are no different from you. You'll meet individuals of all foundations, ages, and nationalities at events called Wordcamps.

All in all, wordpress is not just a constantly improving, easy to use software package, but it is also an ever-evolving online community that is capable of making it better and unique with every passing day. Regardless of whether you are a developer or a layman in software development and installation is concerned, wordpress has something in store for you. So, take the first step and open your doors of learning to wordpress and we can assure you that learning and using wordpress is going to be an enjoyable journey of creation, development and evolution.

GETTING A DOMAIN NAME

Before you get going with website designing and development, there are a few steps that you need to undertake. One of the most crucial of these steps is to set the website up. Don't be bogged down to the technicalities associated with the term 'setup'. It is not as scary as it sounds.

Getting Your Domain Name Registered

One of the first things you require considering the fact that you need to create and maintain a website is to look for a domain name, which in the long run will be the address that users will type to access your website. If you don't know what a domain name is, a domain name is the thing that you write into the address bar of the browser, for example, http://www.facebook.com. A domain name is a unique name that will identify your website and shall be the manner in which anybody from anyplace on the planet can have access to your website.

If you have been able to enroll your domain name successfully, then you're ready to move on to the next step – installing. However, if you are still stuck on this step, the most straightforward path is to get it while you will be signing up for installation. However, you can likewise buy (list) your domain before signing up as well.

There are many spots that you can go to with the end goal to enroll a domain. We commonly suggest Hostgator, Godaddy and Buildawebsite.com. We just suggest Godaddy for space name enlistment, not for hosting. So, don't sign up for installation at the time you register at the event that you pick Godaddy.

To see whether your domain area is accessible, go to a space enlistment center, for example, Godaddy.com. You only need to locate the search box and put your desired website address in it. The provider will allow you options between .com, .info, .org and .net, in addition to several others. Com is the most perceived piece of area, so at whatever point conceivable, get the .com form of your space.

When you discover the name you need and that is accessible, simply follow the steps to finish the enrollment. Always remember, if you are enlisting at Godaddy, don't sign up for anything aside from the space enlistment – disregard the facilitating offers, and so forth that they will reveal to you.

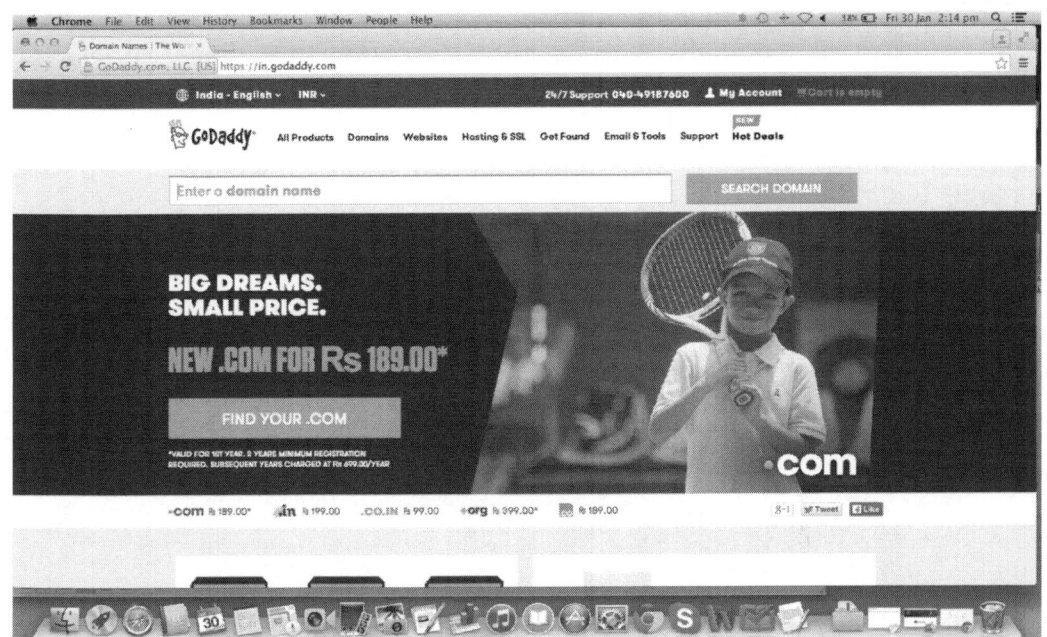

Imagine a scenario where you're not certain what domain name you need. You can't pick between a few you truly like? A decent general guideline is to enroll each of the options. It isn't so much that costly and it provides for you sooner or later to choose. You can start with a certain domain name, and as you move along if you feel that you need a different domain name, it is not difficult to relocate to an alternate space utilizing Backupbuddy. You'll need to have set your choice before you begin advancing your website, yet don't let picking a domain name be one of the hindrance to start.

How To Choose A Domain Name

The legitimate answer is "it depends." You'll likely need to consider organization's name or an expression or question that individuals partner with your site. One of the most critical things that you must consider and remember that the domain name is the first impression of your website and will be the first thing your users will notice about your website. So, be very particular in the decisions you make in this regard.

We generally prescribe enrolling your own individual name as domain too. If you or your organization's names are common, for example, Karl Spenser, you may need to use variations like your full name or a name with a number to make sure that you get a domain related to the name in question.

Some Quick Tips

- Select A Short Name

  The more drew out your URL is, it will make it all the more difficult for your users to remember it. Moreover, it will now be even more probable it is that individuals will incorrectly spell it.

- Choose A Name That Is Easy To Remember

  A string of six arbitrary letters may be truly short, yet it is not simple to recollect. Your domain needs to stick in individuals' personalities with the end goal that it should be easy to recollect, and easy to tell others.

- Remember Your Brand's Identity

  If you have a brand, it is all the more important for you to get a URL that goes well with your brand identity. Individuals will attempt to sort for the sake of your organization with a .com toward the end at any rate, so you should run with it. It is obvious here that you must not use the brand identity of another person or organization as this can work against you. For instance, wordpress is a well known brand and possesses an identity of its own. So, using the name wordpress or a logo similar to the logo of the same is not allowed. Be that as it may you can utilize "press" as has done at pressclub.com.

- Make Use Of Keywords

  Utilizing hunt terms as a component of your name can build your web search tool rankings and expand the possibilities of individuals discovering your webpage. They have to blend well with the names taken commonly, however. For instance, webdevelopment.com incorporates the regular inquiry term "web development," supporting it in natural web index positioning. For this purpose, you will need to figure out a few things. What decisive words would individuals look under so as to discover your kind of business? Will you make use of one or a greater number of keywords yet you must ensure that your name does not sound weird or clumped up in any respect?

- Consider Relevance

  Relevance is a crucial issue and it is important for you to ensure that your website is able to portray its purpose. This is specifically important in view of the fact that you have a business and you will hope to achieve your business objectives. It doesn't need to be enlightening like Google or Amazon is. However, it makes it that much simpler, particularly in case you're not as big a name as these brands.

- Remember That A Domain Name Must Sound Good

  Say your URL so everyone can hear. Now, you must ask them if they can easily spell it out without the need to check the name. On the off chance that somebody tells a companion the URL via telephone would they need to delineate it? Or if you plan out a radio advertisement, will the radio jockey or a listener be able to pronounce and comprehend the name easily?

- Avoid The Use Of Numbers

  The use of numbers in domain names is allowed. However, it is not a recommended practice. The biggest problem that your users will face is that they will not know whether they should spell out the number or use it as a numeral. For instance 7 and seven are the same. This can confuse your target audiences.

- Avoid The Use Of Homophones

  We often use 4 or for and you're for your. In fact, there are many such homophones that have gained excessive popularity lately. Perceive how confounding that can be? When somebody is befuddled, they normally simply proceed onward the following thing, which may in all probability be a rival website.

- Make Sure To Not Use Misspelled Words

Be careful with words that are incorrectly spelled. You may end up buying a misspelled URL and your users. Instead of visiting your website, they will be redirected to the website with the right spelling. You will end up losing traffic and increasing their traffic.

- Remember That Your URL Is A .com

  Remain faithful to the top-level areas, and as a rule, be clear that .com for organizations and .org for philanthropies. There are various types of different choices out there, for example, .biz, .data and .info, yet they're simply not as acknowledged and individuals are liable to sort .com in any case.

  The iPhone incorporates a ".com" catch, which reveals to you exactly how far reaching .coms are. In the event that you do utilize one of alternate sorts of space names, be sure that you are utilizing it for a particular reason.

- Consult

  There may be times that you assume a word or phrase to mean something, but it may mean something else in someone else's dictionary. Therefore, getting an alternate point of view can spare you some shame.

- Do Not Use Letters That Are Hard To Read

  Certain letters beside one another can be tricky to peruse, contingent upon the textual style, in the same way all and i and m, n and r (mnrmnrmnr). Be sure to use words or phrases that can be easily perused.

- Buy Only The Domain You Need And Don't Compromise

  If you have decided on a URL and you feel that it is the most appropriate URL for you. Only to find out that someone else has taken it, then you have the option of buying it from the owner. Although, you may have to pay extra cash for it, if you believe that it is the right URL for you, you must go ahead with the process.

  Also it may be less lavish than you might suspect. Invest eventually conceptualizing and think of loads of thoughts. On the off chance that you have shortlisted a few URLs, you must register each one of them to keep from regretting later. There's nothing more regrettable than investing weeks debating a name. At last choosing and finding that somebody got there before you.

All in all, you just don't need an address, you need an identity for your website. This identity should be in line with your purpose and project you in the right manner globally in view of the fact that online presence has grown to become excessively essential today.

How To Set Up Your Hosting Account

Now that you have got your domain name, the next step is to get a hosting for your website to go live on the Internet and be accessible to the users you are targeting. Consider the term host as a storage space. This storage space will contain all the data related to your website that is visible on the website as well as the data that is required to make your website function. The amount of space you need is directly proportional to the amount of data you have to get your website running.

There are numerous hosting companies that offer you storage space on their server for hosting your website. It is fundamental that you work with the fact that your website will be created on wordpress. This isn't an authority assignment, obviously, simply something we've figured out how to look for through the years. Hostgator is the favored stage of webdesign.com and ithemes. We suggest them owing to their convenience, evaluating, and capacities to host. These make them a preferred host for wordpress destinations.

You can hope to get discounts on Hostgator. However, the amount of discount offered differs on the basis of the time and season of registration. With that said, as a rule, you can hope to get the best deals and most economical options if you take the option of full year registration. The decision is entirely yours. In the event that you know you're beginning something that will last and pass the test of time, then spare a little money by needing a more extended time period.

In the event that your domain name is already registered, maybe one you enlisted at Godaddy.com, you must enter the same on the right hand of the page. However, if you wish to register a domain name now, you must fill it up on the left hand side of the page. Also, make it a point to mention whether you need a .com, .net, .org or any other domain name extension.

You need to click on the location that asks for your payment information. Keep in mind to choose your charging cycle to get the measure of the funds you need. After all the data have been taken, including an exceptional secret key, click "Make Account" and you are en route. Lastly, you will get an email from Hostgator asking for the information that they require to get your wordpress website running.

INSTALLING WORDPRESS

Now that you have a domain name and hosting ready with you, the next obvious step is to install wordpress and get your website up and running. This can be made using two methods – manual installation or using single-click installations offered by Fantastico or any other similar framework. This chapter discusses these options and which one can be employed in which condition.

Using Fantastico For Installing Wordpress

Most companies that offer hosting services offer a "single click installation" of wordpress utilizing cpanel and "Fantastico" or single-click installation using any other platform. Please be advised that it is known as a "single-click" methodology, however there are really around seven steps. Be that as it may, they are all extremely straightforward.

Installation Steps

1. Log into your channel account. You must have been provided the details of this account by the web hosting company that you are registered with.
2. The next step is to look for the Fantastico symbol and click on it.
3. In the following window, click on Wordpress.
4. Now, click on "New Installation"
5. In the following window, finish the establishment's subtle elements and click "Install Wordpress." We emphatically recommend you to not utilize "administrator" as the username for getting to your site. Find something more interesting and harder for another person to figure out. The same principle is applicable for your password. Do you know that values admin and password are the most frequently used words for password and ID or username?
6. Click on the "Completion Installation" catch.
7. Enter your email ID and login points of interest will be emailed to you on the same.

Presently you're good to go! You have a website on an expert server hosted by the organization of your choice. As mentioned previously, your login details will be messages to you. So, be sure to check your email. Also, make it a point to save these details to avoid losing this important data.

Manual Installation

Utilizing Fantastico, or other comparative administrations, is an extraordinary, basic approach to get your wordpress website up and running. The drawback is that it does abandon some security gaps. If security is a concern for you and you have some prior experience of coding for the web and handling databases, manual installation is just your pick. There are some benefits of using the manual method of installation, which are as follows:

1. Following the single-click installation creates database tables with default names and values. Therefore, it is easy for hackers to break into your data, increasing the security concerns considerably. Manual installation allows you full control of the website and database being created.

2. With the help of manual installation, you can completely alter the wp-config.php record, which opens up huge potential in wordpress. Without a doubt, this requires experience and skill on your part to work.

3. It permits you to work inside the "best practices" for security as far as your wordpress website is concerned

If the manual method of installation seems perfect for you, you may need to allude to www.wordpress.org for more directions and detailed steps.

GETTING STARTED WITH YOUR NEW WORDPRESS WEBSITE

The first step once the installation has been completed is to login to the admin panel of your wordpress website. To log into your website, you will need the login credentials that were sent to you by wordpress to your email. Firstly, you need to visit the link:

http://nameofwebsite.com/wp-login.php.

Once you open the link mentioned above, you will be asked to enter your login credentials, which include username and password. Upon input of the values, you must click on the login button. This shall bring you to the dashboard page, which is the admin panel of the website. Here, you can make changes to the website by adding pages, posts, menus and essential website layout.

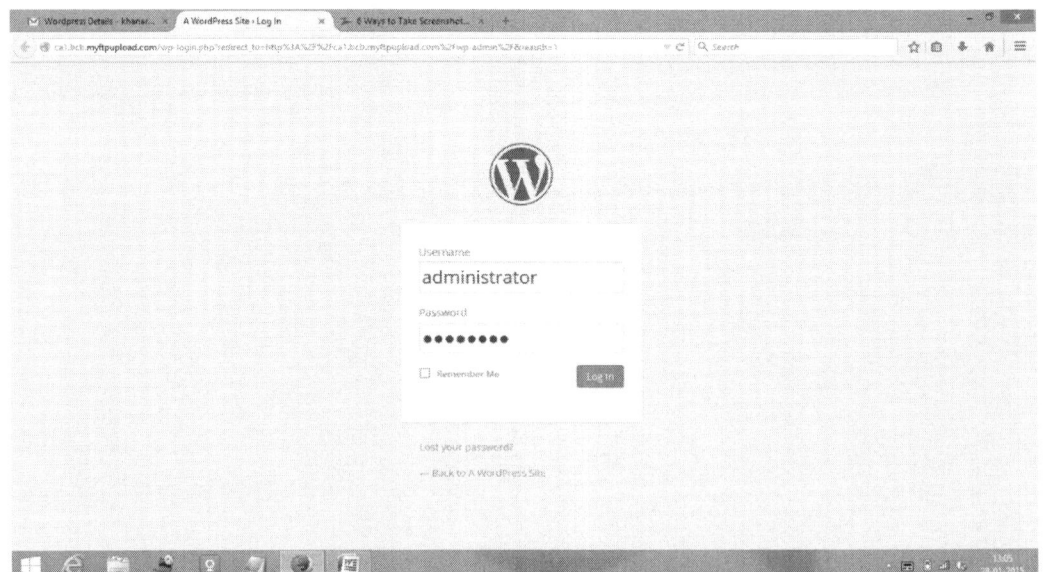

The Wordpress Dashboard

The Dashboard of a wordpress website will discover different dashboard segments, including your website connection, an outline of all the elements that your website will entail, for example, the content (pages, posts, labels and classes) and the discussion components (comments posted on the website, number of comments affirmed, number of comments pending and number of remarks marked as spam). This segment will likewise let you know what subject you are at present utilizing and what variant of wordpress you are utilizing.

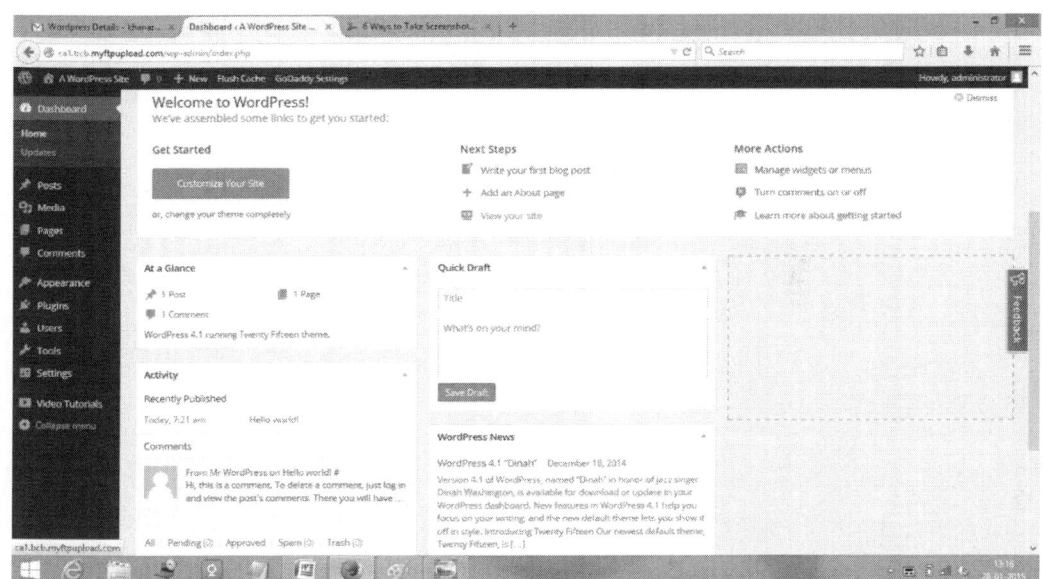

You will likewise discover a segment on comments. This section will give you a better chance to understand what comments are and how you can monitor the same. When you first look at the website page, you will be able to see the list of comments for your website. There are likewise segments telling you what approaching connections you have and wordpress news in the dashboard section. You might likewise have extra segments show up relying upon what plugins you have introduced.

If you closely look at the right half, you will notice a term quickpress on the dashboard. You can utilize this segment to make blog entries straightforwardly from this page. Undoubtedly you will decide to make a post utilizing the directions as a part of a forthcoming segment of this book. You will be able to explore other alternatives. You may also change what you see on your admin page by making changes to the screen options. Closely look at the options available to you and make changes accordingly.

An alternate critical region of your wordpress Dashboard, the range you will utilize is the menu that you see on the left hand side of the admin page. . Here, you will discover connections to the zones where you will include posts and pages, include media, comments, change the presence of your site, get to your subject, include, uproot or upgrade plugins, oversee users, and access devices and settings. If you have installed extra plugins and made changes to the standard wordpress structure, you may see many more options on this left hand menu panel. For instance, in this picture you can see a connection for "Backupbuddy" on the grounds that Backupbuddy is included on this wordpress site of yours.

The Admin Bar

The wordpress Admin bar shows up over your website on the off chance that you are logged into your wordpress dashboard. This is to take into consideration simple altering and website administration specifically from your site without needing to bounce here and there and then here again between the front-end and the back-end. It gives some convenient alternate ways to get to the different aspects of wordpress website. Typically, these are located on the left hand panel of the wordpress admin panel.

It is important to mention here that the admin panel is the admin-specific page and cannot be viewed by the usual readers and users of your website. You can make page-specific changes to the admin page from the profile section. You may change all of the details mentioned in the profile section and save any changes that you have made to implement the same.

Wordpress Settings

The section named Settings on your wordpress admin panel is situated on the left panel of the wordpress admin panel. Precisely, you can locate it closer to the end of the page. When you drift over the "Settings," you will realize that it automatically expands. You may also click on the settings link to expand the settings options.

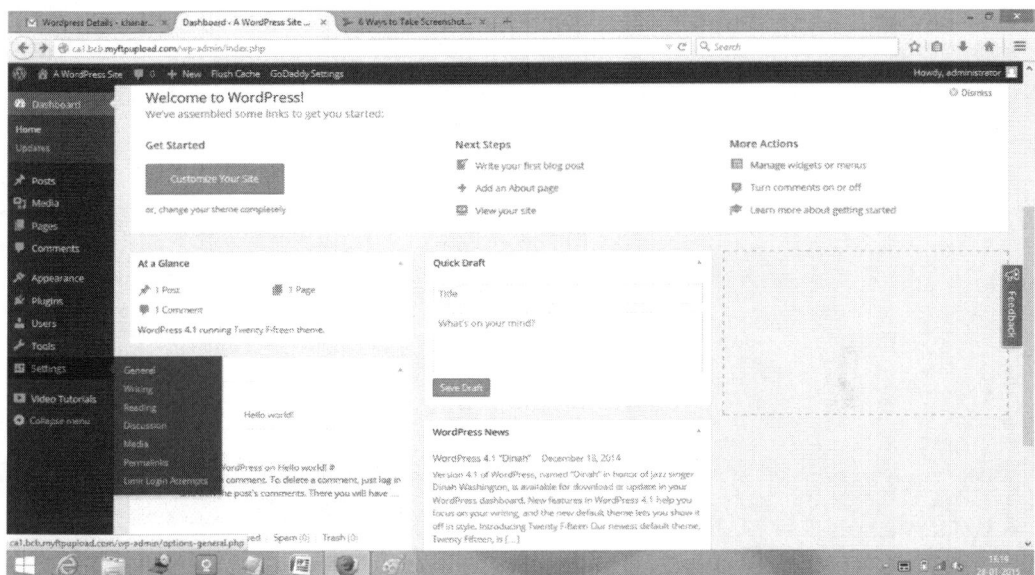

Upon clicking on the settings link, you will see the following screen.

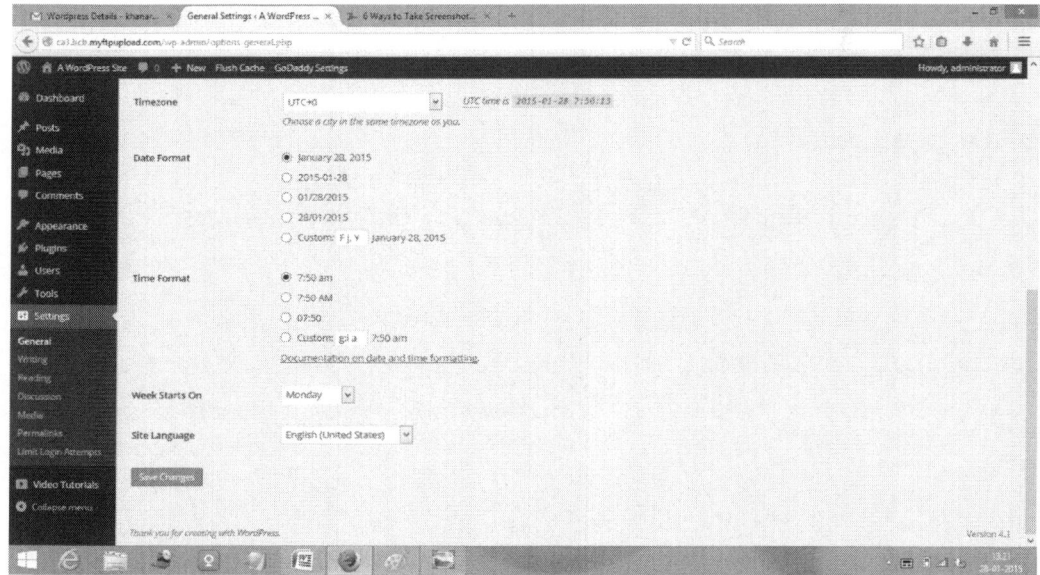

General Settings

The general settings for a website include the website name, tagline and a plethora of other things that you can see on the general settings snapshot. Things, for example, your site name, URL, email, and additionally the time zone data for your site, can be changed from this settings page. When you change these settings, the 'Save Changes' link must be clicked to implement the necessary changes. The option for saving settings can be located as you scroll down to the end of the page.

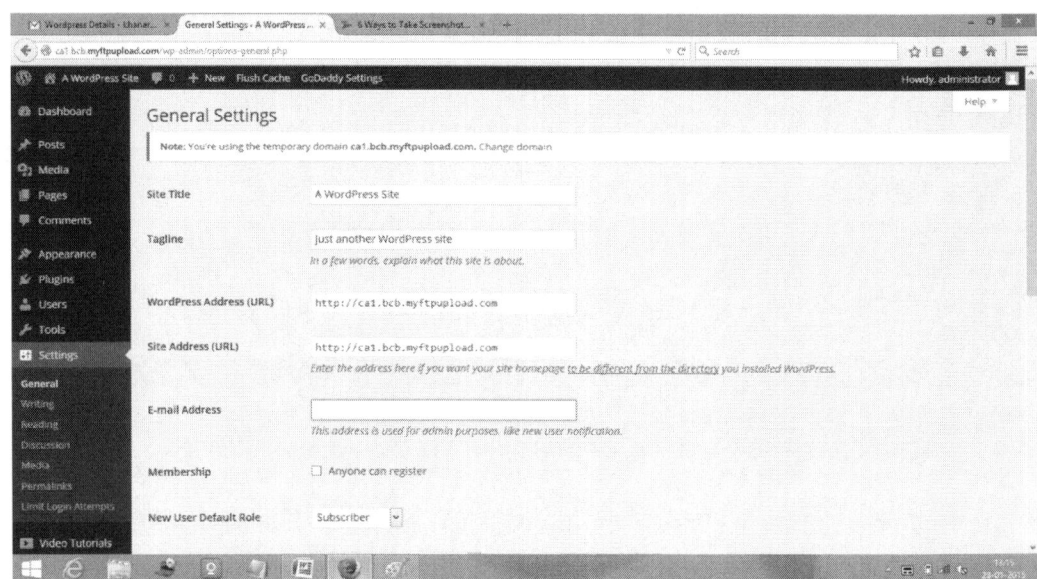

Reading Settings

The settings you choose as part of this section determine your website's user experience. How do you plan to keep your website? Do you want it to be a static page or do you wish to use the chronologically sorted list of blog entries as the front page of your website. You will likewise need to choose what number of blog entries you need to show up on a page before the user needs to see "past posts."

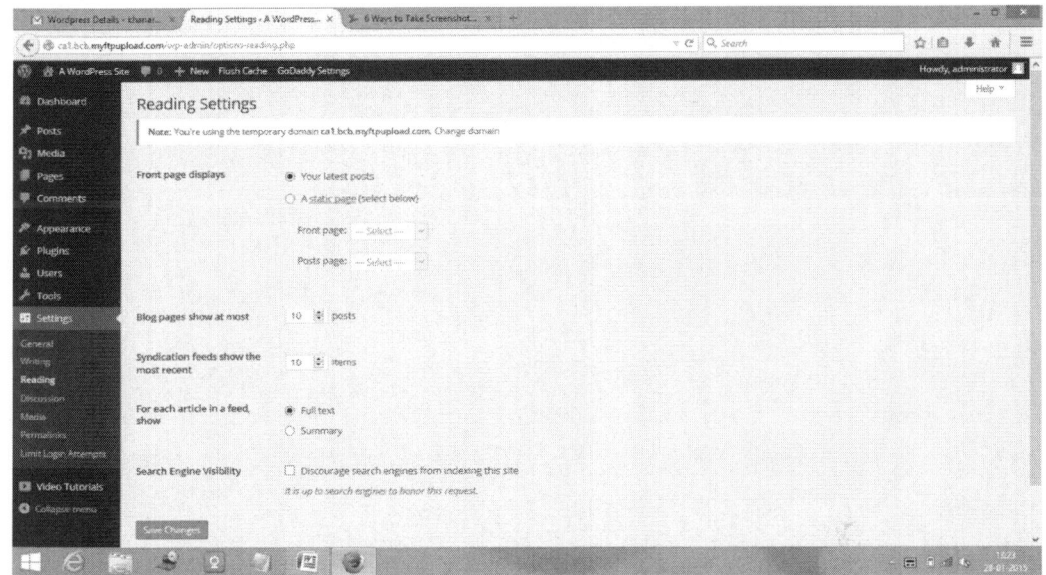

Using Wordpress as a Static Website

In the event that you need to utilize a website as a static content page, then the first things that are of utmost importance to you are the landing pages. If you will be utilizing the site of wordpress, you will need to create an online journal page for showing your blog entries. The title of this page needn't be web journal. You can keep it anything you like.

In order to set the settings for this purpose, you just need to go to the reading setting and select the checkbox against static page. The system will automatically ask you to enter the page that you would like to set as the static page for the front page and the page that would display the blog entries. If you don't wish to use a web journal page, you can just leave the settings as it is.

Settings for Writing

This webpage of the admin panel allows you to determine the amount of freedom and convenience that writers to your page will have. For instance, it determines what will be the default category of your posts and whether you can create a post through email or any other remote options.

Media Settings

As far as media settings are concerned, you must have noticed that many people prefer to set them to the default settings. However, you may observe that you need your picture classifications – large, medium, thumbnail – to be not the same as the default settings. Moreover, you can also determine the location at which all your media files will be located. Of course, they will transfer to the wp-content/transfers folder.

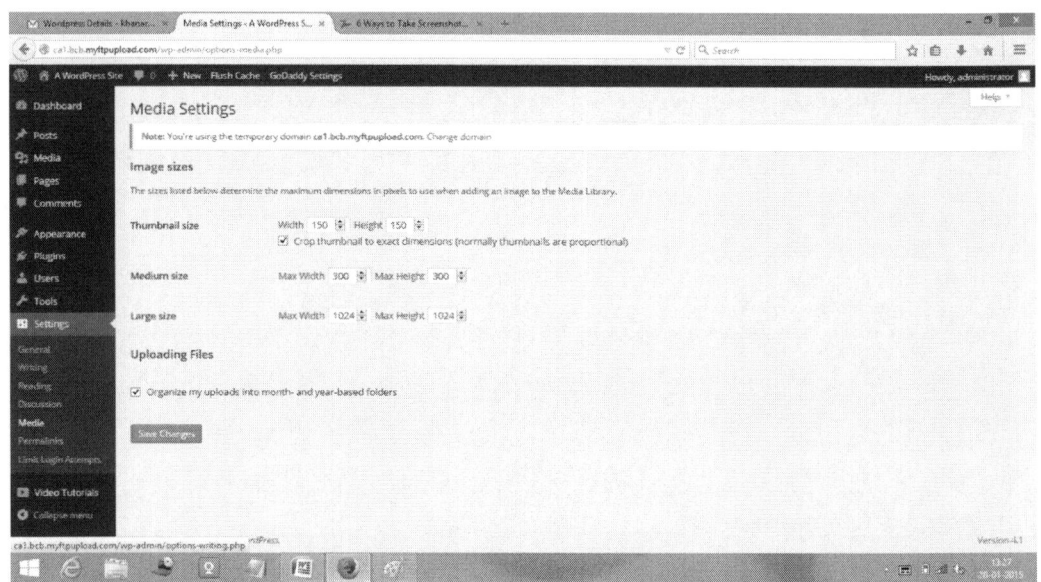

Settings for Discussion

If you are wondering how you can manage the comments settings for your website, then discussion settings are your answer. You'll have the capacity to figure out if remarks can post naturally. You may choose whether comments will need your approval before going live or post on their own. Select your settings here painstakingly as they will influence how other people see your website.

You will likewise have the capacity to recognize words, IP addresses, phrases, names, email addresses and URLs that you need to "boycott" from having the capacity to make remarks on your site. Moreover, you can choose how – or if –

you need the commentator's portrait (symbol) to show up alongside their remark.

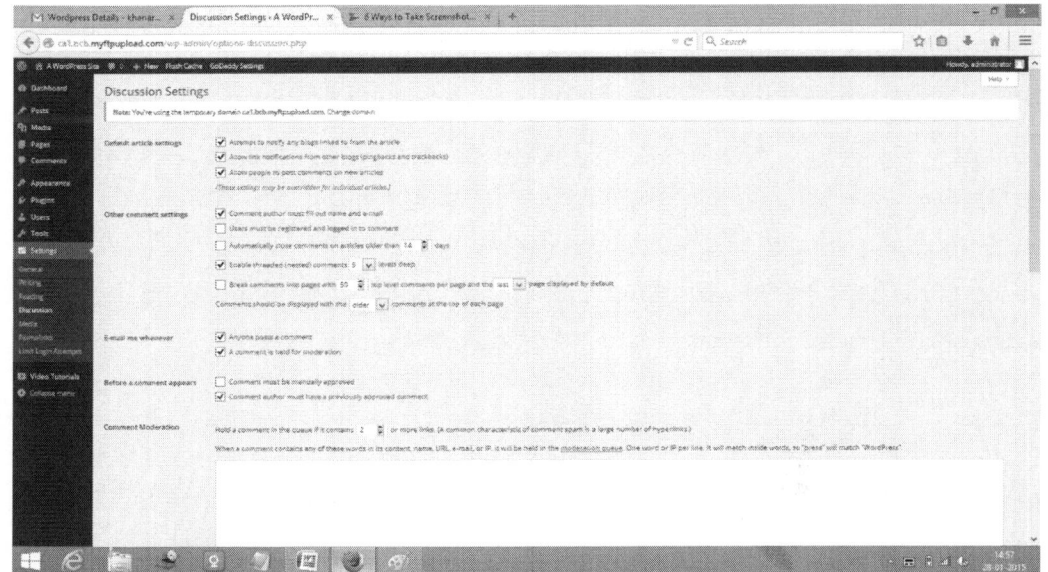

Security Settings

These settings are particularly helpful on the off chance that you are creating your site and possess no clue as to what you should do to make your website visible to the world. Essentially, select the proper radio catch and Save Changes. It is vital to note here that on the off chance that you choose "Ask web crawlers not to index this webpage." Ensure that you have the right settings installed on your website to improve and increase your visibility to the Internet world or else no one will ever know how much effort you had put to make your website.

Setting the Permalinks

Permalinks hold importance in your website in view of the fact that it impacts both your website look and SEO relevance. Permalinks may be described as the link, which is essentially changeless and directs you to the website page being called. This is also the link that your users and other websites will use to connect with your website's pages. By default, wordpress makes permalinks that are short of help. They have inquiry checks and a bunch of numbers that are totally insignificant to the normal client. They resemble this:

http://www.samplewebsite.com/?p=112

That jumbled wreckage isn't useful to anyone, including web indexes. These links contain a number, which is the content identification number as saved in the wordpress database. These links can easily take users to the content directed, but at the same time they don't tell the user – or web search tools – all that much, henceforth they aren't extremely helpful. A basic change is to make your permalinks easy to understand. Valuable permalinks resemble this:

http://www.samplewebsite.com/about-me

That makes your links a considerable measure more helpful. It enhances the feel, ease of use and similarity of the links. It's not just useful for people taking a gander at connections, yet it can likewise help your Internet searcher positioning. Having genuine words in the URL, particularly your content's keywords, is a great website streamlining (SEO) procedure.

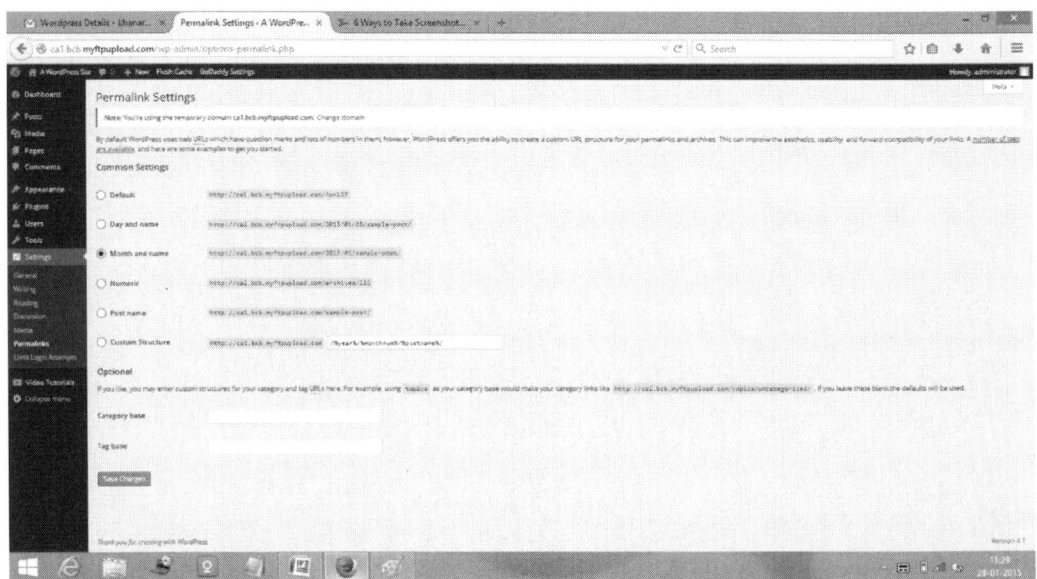

These enhanced, client and web search tool benevolent permalinks are frequently called pretty permalinks. What's more, it is not difficult to utilize them as a part of wordpress. Setting Your Permalinks from the wordpress dashboard is rather simple. You just need to go to Settings -> Permalinks. This allows you to set the permalink settings as you desire. The 'Post name' setting will provide you a basic URL like this:

http://www.samplewebsite.com/post-title

If SEO friendly permalink is your priority, simply select 'Post name'. The Custom Structure field will show up the new configuration. Keep in mind to save changes before moving on. Several permalink configurations are available for you to use. However, by and large, simplicity is the key. You must implement the permalink policy that is the simplest.

PAGES AND POSTS

At the point, when making content for your wordpress site, there are two fundamental sorts of these: Posts and Pages. This chapter discusses the different aspects of these two fundamental content forms that you will create, edit, remove and work around with.

A wordpress post is the thing that makes up the "online journal" part of your website. These are for the most part news or instructive overhauls. Typically recorded in converse ordered request the most current posts appear at the top. They can be labeled, arranged and filed.

This content will be found on the landing page as your essential content, or a "web journal" page. Therefore, it can be used for making up your site's RSS content. For most locales, you'll consistently include new posts, making an element, redesigning stream of content always.

On the other hand, a wordpress page is for the most part saved for static data, in the same way as content is saved for other pages like the about me page. Therefore, this content is not recorded by date and will typically show up in the site's menu. They can't be labeled, arranged or chronicled by date. Moreover, this content is excluded in your site's RSS channel.

Utilizing Posts & Pages

For the most part, website content entails the posts that are published on the website. On the other hand, pages are utilized for standalone data that isn't overhauled regularly. For instance, an association may utilize posts for handling news overhauls, press releases, work postings or new items. Anyhow, they'd utilize pages to rundown "about" data, administrations, contact information, group bios, areas or local laws. Wordpress is adaptable and posts and pages can be used anyway, you need yet this provides for you an essential outline of how they function.

How To Create Posts

To make a post on your site, go to Posts >Add New. If you are unable to find this option, you can find it in the left hand section menu of the admin page. The top of the page will ask you to enter a page title. For a new post, this text box will inevitably say, "Enter title here." In the snapshot shown below, you can see the content creation section of this admin page.

If you look at the right hand section of this page, you will notice the publish button. It also allows you to save the post as a draft, which you can publish at a later time. You can see a percentage of alternate choices, including arrangement, classes and labels, in addition to several others. We will cover those in more detail later. Obviously, you have options galore as far as post creation is concerned. However, we have discussed the basics, which must be enough to get started with post creation.

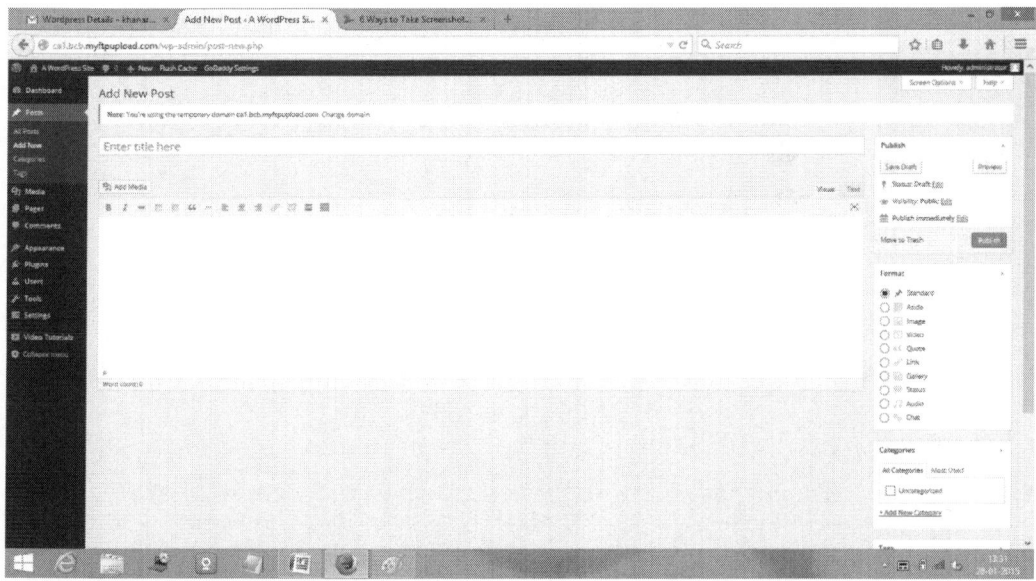

You can likewise turn off alternatives that you don't wish to utilize. You don't have to stress over the different options that are available to you. However, it is always good to know about all the options that you have and how you can switch each of these off or activate the same as and when needed. Now and again it is simpler to turn off components you're not utilizing so they don't occupy you.

How To Create Pages

In order to make a page on your site, you need to go to Pages > Add New in the left menu. You may perceive that making a page looks a great deal like making a post. Content creation page for these two types of content is the same because both are essentially content that will be displayed on the website. Although, there are obvious similarities between these two types of content and how they are created, there are some differences as well. One of the visible differences is the mention of the terms category and tag for the page.

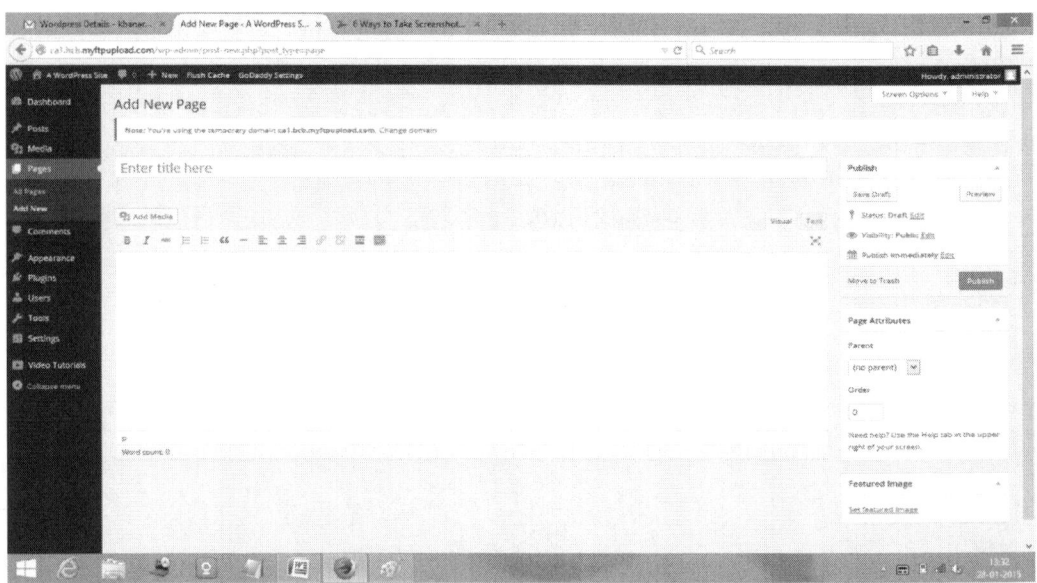

You can see at the top of the page that the content creation form requests you to enter the title. Below that is the fundamental substance zone where you can compose the substance of the page. In the publish box on the right, you can see saving options and publishing options for the page concerned.

An important difference between pages and posts is page attributes. This region permits you to provide for some request, or setting, to your pages. You can also set the page hierarchy by declaring whether a page is a child page of an existing page or not. This declaration plays an important role in determining the position of the page on the website menu.

Unlike posts, pages are not saved with time-stamps and can be associated with categories, tags or hierarchy. It is possible to set the page as a child page of an already created page using the page attributes section. For instance, on the off chance that you were including an about area, you'd make the about page. This will be the parent page. If you create pages like Team, History and Foundation, you can declare these pages as child pages of the about page.

For starters, you need to create a page, which will be declared as the parent page. If your parent page is not already declared, it will not show up the dropdown against the parent page setting. Therefore, child page is the page that declares an existing page as its parent page. When you make your site's menu, you'll have the capacity to effortlessly mastermind hierarchy that you want your website to follow and the same will be visible in the website menu.

This method can be particularly helpful in managing and organizing your website content. It also allows you to control the number of elements that will exist on your menu and how the same will be laid out. For instance, if you declare three pages as child pages of a parent page, these will appear under the parent page in the main menu. The end user will be able to see these child pages links when he or she hovers over the parent page link. The menus can be altered using the menu settings, which will be discussed in the chapter on menus.

You can also decide the layout of the page by setting the page attributes of the page concerned. This shall allow you to customize your website at an altogether different level and give different looks to the same set of pages. Before you start looking for these options in your admin panel, be sure to understand that the availability of these settings are theme-dependent.

So, if your theme does not support these settings, you will not be able to make changes to them. You have various sorts of designing choices when you're making a wordpress page or post. When you are creating content, you can avail all the options that are accessible on the top bar of the content creation window.

What Is The Visual Editor

Naturally, wordpress utilizes a visual editor. This visual editor is also known as a WYSIWYG editor. The full form of this weirdly huge acronym is 'What You See Is What You Get'. That implies you don't have to know the code to set the configuration of your post. It meets expectations much the same as Microsoft Word. You have the option of making something striking, highlight your content and click on the "B" to make the content bold.

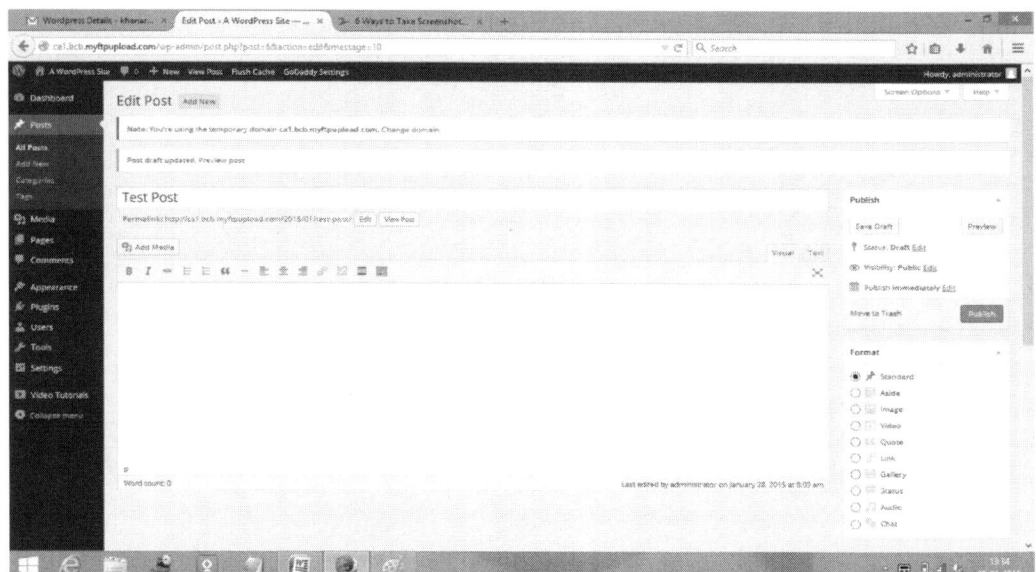

Here are all the arranging alternatives:

- Bold

  This setting allows you to create striking content and is most useful for segment sub-heads and highlighting essential focuses.

- Italics

  This setting allows you to emphasize content. Boldness is best utilized for book titles.

- Strikethrough

  This setting crosses out content as if you have struck it off manually. This setting is most beneficial to be used with text where you want to include the text, but you don't want it to be an active part of the text used. So, it will be printed, but it will be crossed out.

- Unordered List

  You must have seen that many people also refer to this type of list using the term bulleted list. This is a decent approach to present a concise and precise view of your data. It's additionally a decent approach to make large content concise, which adds to the readability of your content.

- Ordered List

  If the data you wish to display needs to be ordered, then the best way to represent your lists is in the form of ordered lists. This will naturally number every section in your rundown, making it uncomplicated to retreat and include things or rework them without needing to re-number them.

- Block quote

  An uncommon approach to haul out and highlight content, generally a more extended quote. The appearance of block quotes is determined by the theme installed for the wordpress website.

- Align Left/Align Center/Align Right

  No astonishments here, these choices will adjust your content's alignment to left, right or left and right.

- Adding and Editing Links

  You can add or remove links to your content using this functionality. We will discuss this topic in greater detail in the sections to follow.

- Insert More

  When you have too much content to be displayed for a small section, it is a good practice to display a set number of characters and add a read more link at the end of display. This affects how your posts show up on the landing page, class, label and document pages. Upon clicking the read more links, the user shall be redirected to the full post page. This is a decent instrument to use on more posts, permitting readers to get a piece of the post, yet less that it overpowers them. It makes your landing page and documents pages simpler to span through and check.

- Spellcheck

This one's really clear and convenient, as well! You can likewise utilize the dropdown beside the spellcheck to get to spellcheck for diverse dialects.

- Fullscreen Mode

  If you need to make posts with lesser preoccupations, this is the alternative for you. It drops off the greater part of the standard wordpress route components and simply gives you a chance to spotlight on composing your post.

- Show/Hide Kitchen Sink

  There is a considerable measure of designing alternatives, yet they're covered up. This choice will uncover all the arranging decisions the 'everything and the kitchen sink' alternatives. Designing bar pairs in tallness with an entirely new column of arranging choices. All the accompanying organizing choices are covered up in the 'kitchen sink' alternatives. Click on 'Show Kitchen Sink' to uncover the second line of alternatives, which have been discussed below.

- Format

  The first choice permits you to add HTML content to your page or post. Anyway don't stress if you don't have to know HTML. The default setting is passage and will be set for the general content that you publish. There are a few different alternatives including location, pre-formatted text and six separate sizes of headers.

- Underline

  This setting lets you underline content. Utilize this setting sparingly as the favored approach is to use italics. This setting is used to emphasize the content used for titles and underline the text that is used as a link.

- Alignment

  Alignment determines the position of your text with respect to other elements of the webpage. You can choose to align your text left, center and right.

- Text Color

  The editor given with content creation form allows you to pick the color of the content that will be published. This is another option that must be utilized sparingly.

- Pasting Content

  You can paste content using two methods: as plain text and as formatted text. Pasting as plain text will strip out the additional characters and undetectable garbage that is frequently replicated when you duplicate content. Microsoft Word includes additional coding when you simply duplicate the content, so utilizing the pasting method that pastes from the word software removes all coding and formatting marks included in the text. As a dependable guideline, however, we suggest replicating from a content record, or writing specifically into the editorial manager window, instead of duplicating from Word.

- Remove Formatting

  This is a convenient approach to get rid of all formatting including striking, italics, colors, and so forth, from a piece of content in one snappy step.

- Inserting a Custom Character

  Assorted types of uncommon characters can be inserted that don't show up on your console utilizing this choice, including dashes, copyright images and many more.

- Indenting Text

  You can indent text by using this formatting feature.

- Undo/Redo

  Just like you do in word, redoing and undoing content changes, is also possible in the content creation form of wordpress. You can use this option for accomplishing the same.

- Help

  You may not be able to memorize everything about these alternatives and options. This option will open some help alternatives particularly identified with making posts.

The HTML Editor

If you are acquainted with HTML coding, you will like to see the HTML equivalent to be better equipped to take control of what your website has on display. You can view the HTML equivalent of the displayed text by changing content tabs. This tab can be seen at the top-right corner of the content creation region. This perspective will demonstrate the genuine code of your blog entry. You can compose your post here in the event that you need yet, you have to incorporate the code rather than simply utilizing visual proofreader's helpful arranging catches. Lastly, this feature is a great way to gain control over what you display and have displayed on your website.

Scheduling Posts

One of the extraordinary accommodations of wordpress is having the capacity to calendar your posts to go live at whatever time you need. It may appear like an essential gimmick, yet numerous online journal frameworks just give you a chance to distribute a post in a flash. Planning each post is an incredible approach to position and format your content. It is also a great way to verify you're reliably posting material.

In wordpress, you have the option to publish instantly or at a scheduled time on the calendar. Clicking on the publish button will publish your post instantly. However, you can also choose to schedule your post by choosing the date and time of publishing from the calendar-time tool given below the publish button.

Including Links

You include a link by basically highlighting the content you need to connect and select the connection symbol from the rundown of symbols in your manager window. A crate will pop up requesting that you enter the objective URL. Include the URL and you're ready. Make certain to incorporate the "http://" toward the start of the URL. Therefore, it is advisable to copy and paste the URL from the Internet browser itself.

You can likewise add a discretionary title to your connection. The title is the text that will appear only when a user hovers the mouse over the link. Here, you can also decide if you want your linked page to open in another tab or a new window. If need be, you can link your content to the content of the same page as well. For this, you will have to look for 'link to content on the same page' in the options.

This shall improve readability of your content and enhance the overall user experience of your website. Always remember that links are an important tool in the website world. So, if you are able to use them wisely, you can benefit your website immensely. Each time you include a connection you're including useful associations between content.

You ought to likewise be particular in what words you decide to connect. It's regularly useful to make the clearest words the connection. Connected content frequently emerges in an alternate shade. For instance, links are underlined. So, you must ensure that the text you put for the link is relevant and directs the user to the right piece of information. The real content that is connected additionally helps Internet searchers get to the content they want. You are also more likely to rank better in searches and position better in your SEO plan.

Including Images

Pictures or images can be included into posts or pages by using the 'add or upload' option in the formatting bar. You can likewise add any type of media using this option. You can pick pictures in three ways, which are described below:

From Computer

This is the most widely recognized approach to add photographs to your site. You can either drag them specifically to the transfer screen or click 'Select Files' to pick a file from your machine. When the picture is transferred, you can alter a percentage of the settings for the picture.

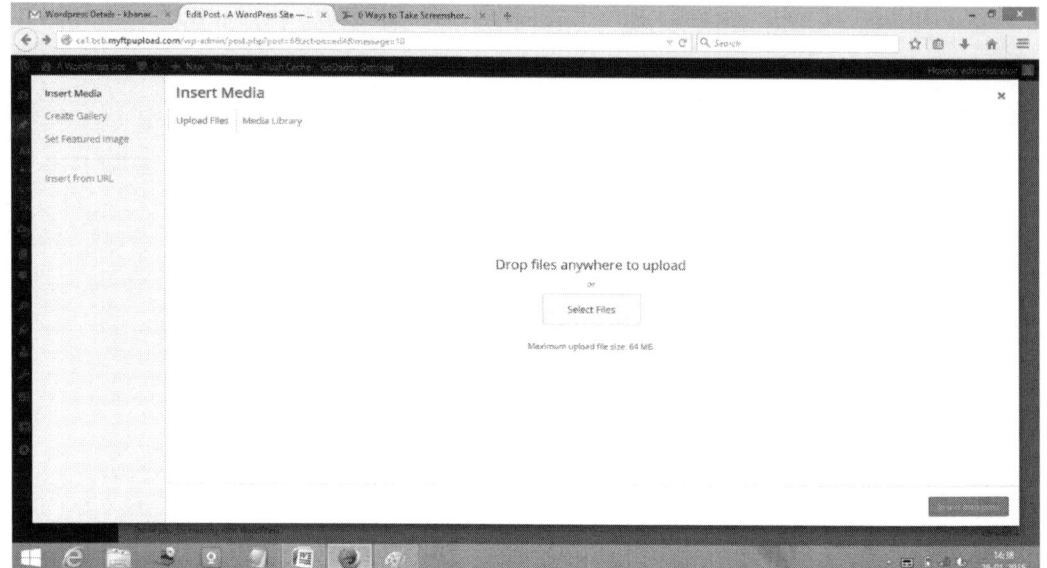

These settings include:

- Title

  This is obliged, but at the same time it is consequently created from the record name. It will show up as content when a guest drifts over the picture with the mouse.

- Alt Text

  This is the content that shows up when a picture hasn't stacked and is utilized by site users for the outwardly hindered. It is additionally perused via Internet searchers, so consider the use of keywords when you are picking your alt content.

- Description

  This is content that will show straightforwardly underneath your image.

- Link URL

  What the picture will connect to will be described by the link URL. Inevitably, this link will connect to the full size variant of the picture. You can likewise enter your own particular connection or no connection.

- Alignment

  Where you need the picture located and how do you want it to align itself with respect to other elements on the webpage.

- Size

    The dimensions of the picture shown to the user are given by size. Wordpress will naturally make a few sizes for you to browse. At times, it is useful to put a little picture on a webpage. This thumbnail size picture can be linked to its full size counterpart so that readers can have a better look at the picture if they want. You can likewise click 'Alter Image' to turn, flip, crop, or scale the picture. You must click 'Embed into Post' when you are prepared to include your picture in the post or page.

From URL

An alternate choice is to utilize a picture that shows up on an alternate site. As opposed to transferring the picture to your site, you're simply going to connect to it on an alternate site. Since the picture dwells somewhere else and you're simply connecting to that area, if the picture is relocated for whatever reason, it will not be available to you anymore.

Simply enter the URL for the picture and add in data that is described previously. Note that you can't pick distinctive sizes or alter the picture. This is the case simply because it is not yours and you have no right to alter it. A quick tip for you here is that if the picture is put at another location, be sure to take permission from the author or copyright owner of the image before attempting to use it personally or commercially.

Media Library

The last choice for adding pictures is to pick a picture you've officially transferred to your site. The media library contains all these pictures. You can seek through the pictures in your Media Library and after that click the "Show" interface on the panel. At that point, you can alter a percentage of the picture's settings and add it to the page or post.

CATEGORIES AND TAGS

You can allot a post to numerous classes or categories, yet you must dole out a post for no less than one of the available categories. Naturally, a post will be allocated to the "Uncategorized" classification. This is the case if you do not assign any category to your newly published post. Fortunately, you can change the category of your posts by going through Post -> Categories alternative in your Wordpress dashboard.

You can allot classes to the privilege of your entrance. Simply click on a class to choose it. You can likewise make another classification using 'Add New Category' at the base. For this, you just need to add the name of the new category and click on the add button below.

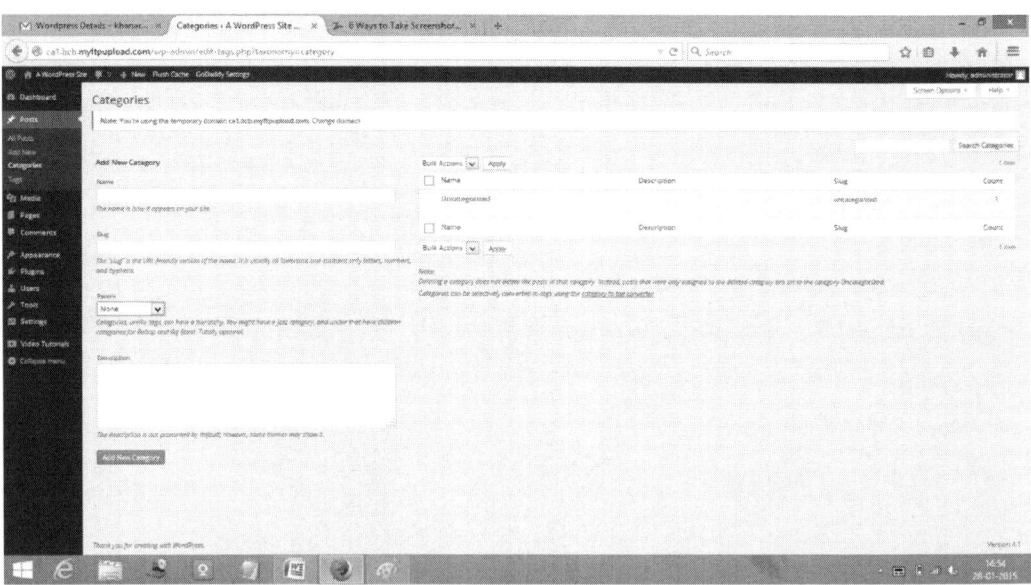

Categories can likewise be sorted out progressively with sub-classifications. Wordpress also gives you the option to create a hierarchy of categories. Whenever you create a new category, you may select a parent category to disclose its parentage and place in the hierarchy. Moreover, if the number of categories you are working with is rather high, you have the most used categories filter to bail you out of the situation.

On the other hand, tags can also be added to your post beneath the categories. You can allocate the same number of tags, as you need, however by and large you would not like to relegate too much. Five to ten are presumably the most extreme. Not at all like categories, tags are totally discretionary.

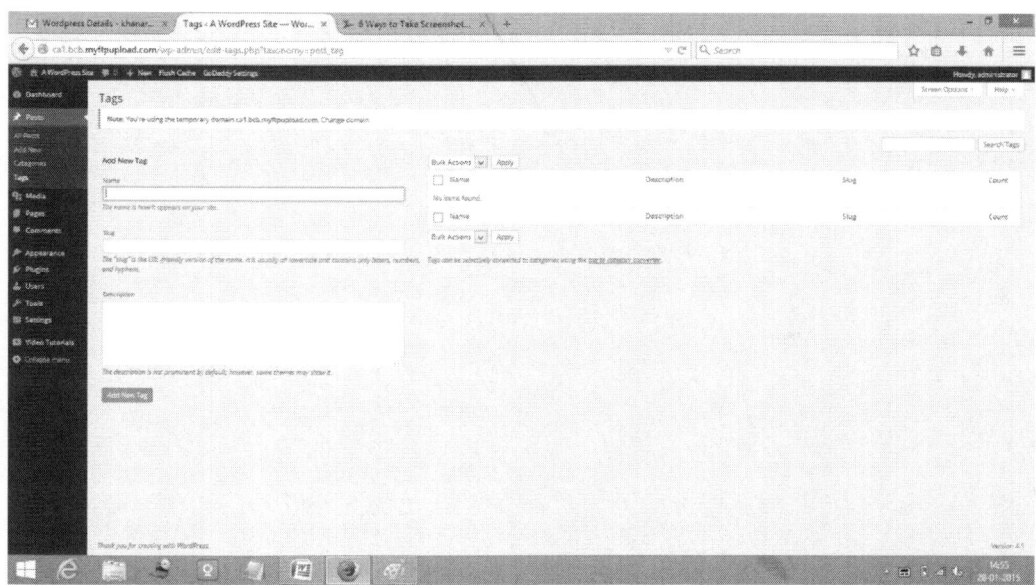

All that you need to do here is add the name of the tag and click on add. Enter a few tags without a moment's delay by differentiating them with commas. You can likewise browse the most utilized tags. You also possess the option to remove tags. Each tag has a cross, made in front of it. You just need to click on the cross to remove the tag concerned. It is important to mention here that tags do not comprehend cases. So, my and My mean the same in the tags world.

You can utilize your tags and categories any way you need, yet by and large tags are more particular than categories. Most locales utilize categories to portray general subjects. To comprehend this concept, let us take the example of a Facebook post. The category for such a post will be social networking. However, the tag is something more precise and most likely should take the value Facebook. Labels ought to all the more particularly characterize the post, while categories simply give a general subject. This is particularly useful to your users in the event that they're keen on a particular subject.

In the event that they loved your post about Facebook upgrades, for instance, they could undoubtedly discover more posts on your site about online networking or all the more particularly about Facebook. Utilizing categories and tags is a decent approach to help users find more data and invest additional time burrowing through your website's content.

PLAYING AROUND WITH PLUGINS

Wordpress Plugins are bits of programming that augments the capacities of wordpress. They offer you a chance to derive much more from your basic web journal website, even if you are not making a web journal. Since wordpress is open source programming, these are all outside instruments that allow extra functionality to what Wordpress can do. They're not difficult to download and install on your system. However, most of these plugins are free of charge, a few premium plugins may cost you money so that you can download, install and use them.

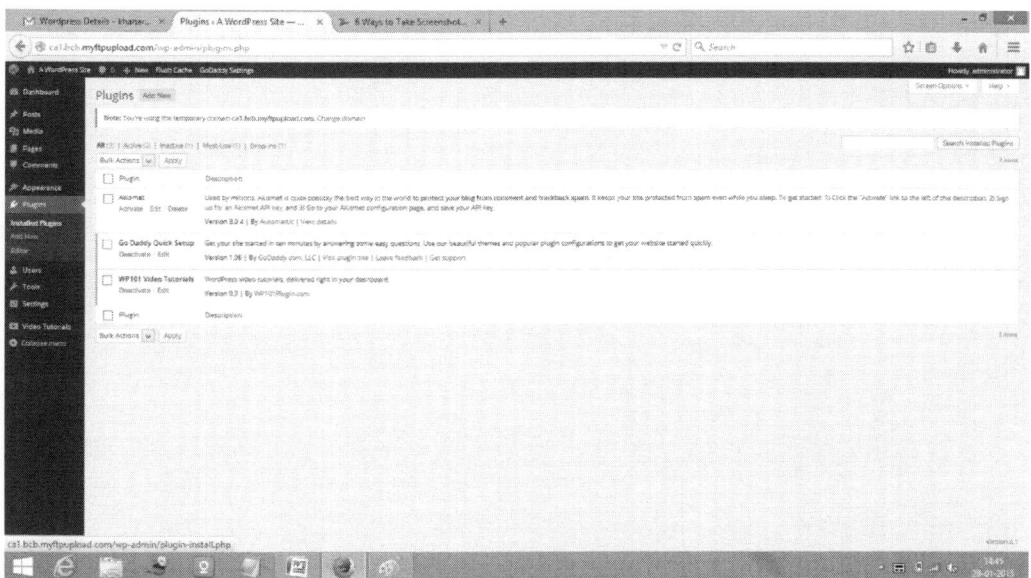

Plugins can do things like enhance your site rankings; showcase related posts in your sidebar, do complete reinforcements of your Wordpress website or make staggering web structures rapidly and effortlessly. You can add pretty much any functional ability to wordpress with plugins. The biggest advantage that wordpress offers you is its huge online community backup. Everything and anything that this community contributes as far as plugins are concerned is added to the Wordpress Plugin Directory, which makes it a rich reservoir of plugins. As of now, there are more than 18,000 plugins in the wordpress index, so there's a considerable measure to browse.

How to Install Plugins

It's not difficult to add and install new plugins to your existing wordpress website. You just need to go to Plugins -> Add New and you will get your set of choices. Basically, you have two options as far as searching and installing plugins are concerned. You can follow any one of these methodologies for solving your purpose.

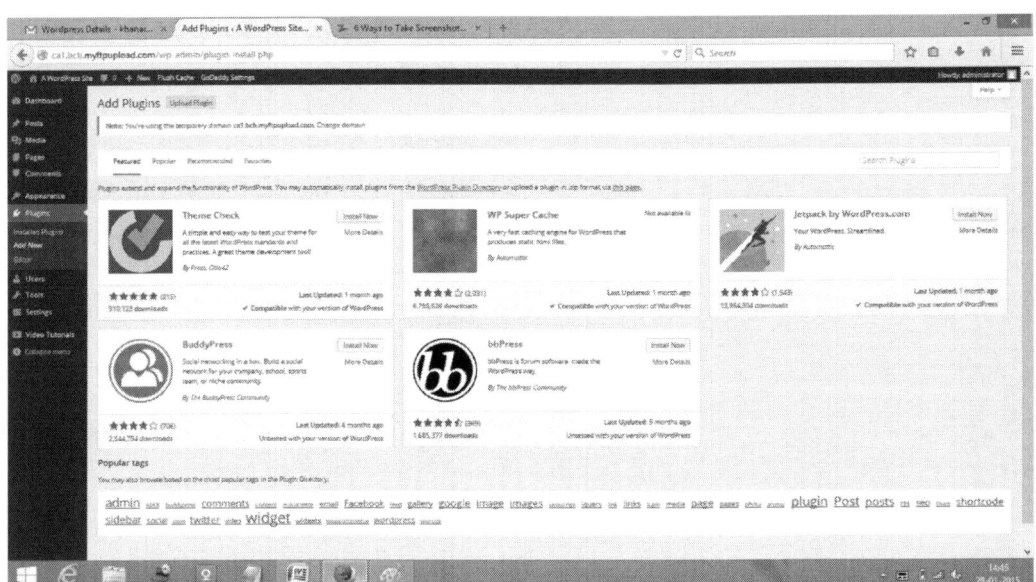

Look and Install

The first methodology is to look for the plugin by searching through the directory. The available plugin can then be used for installation and use. Your first choice is to look for the plugin you need in the Wordpress Plugin Directory. You can discover a plugin and install the same from here. Once the plugin is introduced, simply click "activate." You may require the login data for your site's host to complete installation of plugins. This data can be taken from the web host and it may be the same data that you had used for setting up wordpress.

Download and Install

The second alternative that you can use is download and install. As part of this, you first need to download the plugin from any source other than the wordpress directory. It will typically come as compressed package. If you look at the plugins page, you will see a link that says, 'Add New.' Clicking on this link shall take you to a page that allows you to add plugins. Once you have downloaded and installed the plugin, you simply need to click on activate to get going.

Manual Installation

Plugins can also be installed using manual installation, which uses FTP for upload and install of the same. The manual installation is a little more complex and if you are a novice, you may not want to try your hands on this one. This method requires you to manually upload the compressed file containing the plugin. Utilizing a FTP project and transferring the plugin file to the wp-content/plugins envelope on your site can do this. At this point, if you go to the plugins page that lists all the plugins installed, you will find the name of the recently installed plugin as well. Finally, you need to click 'Activate' the plugin to get started.

Picking Plugins

With such a large number of plugins out there, it is useful to comprehend a bit about how they're composed and how the methodology functions. For one thing, the Wordpress Plugin Directory is the best hotspot for nothing plugins. These plugins have been verified by the Wordpress group to guarantee there are no pernicious plugins or detestable code. Anyhow that doesn't mean each plugin in the catalog meets expectations flawlessly. However, it is important to mention here that some of these may not work as expected and that is a risk that comes with their being free of cost.

Remember this as you peruse the index. A few plugins may be quite a while old and haven't been upgraded. They may work fine and dandy. Then again they may cause numerous kinds of issues. Simply be mindful about the plugin you are adding to your website and don't be astonished on the off chance that you have to erase a plugin and discover another one. It's additionally a decent thought to introduce one plugin at once and check your website after every establishment. That way if your website breaks, it is not difficult to identify the plugin that has led to the condition or is expected to lead to a condition and you can simply remove it from your wordpress account.

Be mindful of the fact that even though a plugin comes for free, someone has put in the time and effort to create it. So remember that when you utilize a free plugin. It's great practice to think about making as a gift to the engineer when you utilize one of their free plugins. This is a decent approach to say much appreciated and help them proceed with their advancement work.

Some plugins may not perform in the manner that they should. So, you can contact the online community to seek help on your issues. The engineer is not committed to bail you out. Be sensible when you request help and be appreciative for what you get. On the off chance that you do wind up requiring and getting backing from a designer, that is the time to make a gift and demonstrate your appreciation. Don't be a moocher.

Since there are such a variety of plugins out there, it is essential not to try too hard. It's not difficult to continue attaching plugins to your site, yet every one eases your site off. A few plugins will even cover, with diverse plugins doing likewise work. Lastly, only use the plugins that you need and if you have any extra plugins installed on your machine, be sure to remove them as soon as they lose relevance on your website

Premium Plugins

If you feel that none of the free plugins are offering the kind of functionality you require, then you must take a look at the premium plugins before going for custom coding. These are professionally planned plugins you pay a charge for. By and large, you're not so much paying only for the plugin, however for the expert, quality help that accompanies it.

Also numerous premium plugins are all out powerhouses, supercharging wordpress in ways you'd never anticipate. Some of these plugins make wordpress far beyond a blogging stage that it is no astonishment you have to pay for them. Things like transforming your site into an out and out e-business arrangement with Cart66 or Shopp. It took somebody a great deal of time to compose that code and remain in line with what is going on in the wordpress world. Therefore, it must not be surprising that they get paid for it. At times, that plugin may be somebody's business. At last, the decision you need to make on your part is to discover the plugins that work for your site, whether they you are using the free ones or you paid for them.

Backupbuddy

Backupbuddy takes into account simple reinforcement, reclamation and movement of your website. Everyone has heard loathsomeness stories where a machine passed on and somebody lost everything on the grounds that they didn't have a backup in place. This situation can just as much affect your website as well. In any case, Backupbuddy offers true serenity. It's a decent speculation to protect the time and exertion you put into making and maintaining your wordpress site.

ADDING SUBSTANCE TO WEBSITES WITH THEMES

You can change the complete look, feel and default functionality of a website by changing the theme or template used by your website. Themes is a concept that allows you to control the design of your website completely without having the need to hire a designer. Therefore, whenever you feel the need to change the look of the website without having to make changes in the backend programming or data of the website, you can go with a new theme.

Wordpress themes are somewhat like how another outfit can provide for you a totally new look. At the same time, topics go much deeper than simply the configuration. They control the format and usefulness of your site also. You can make distinctive designs for diverse sorts of content with a theme.

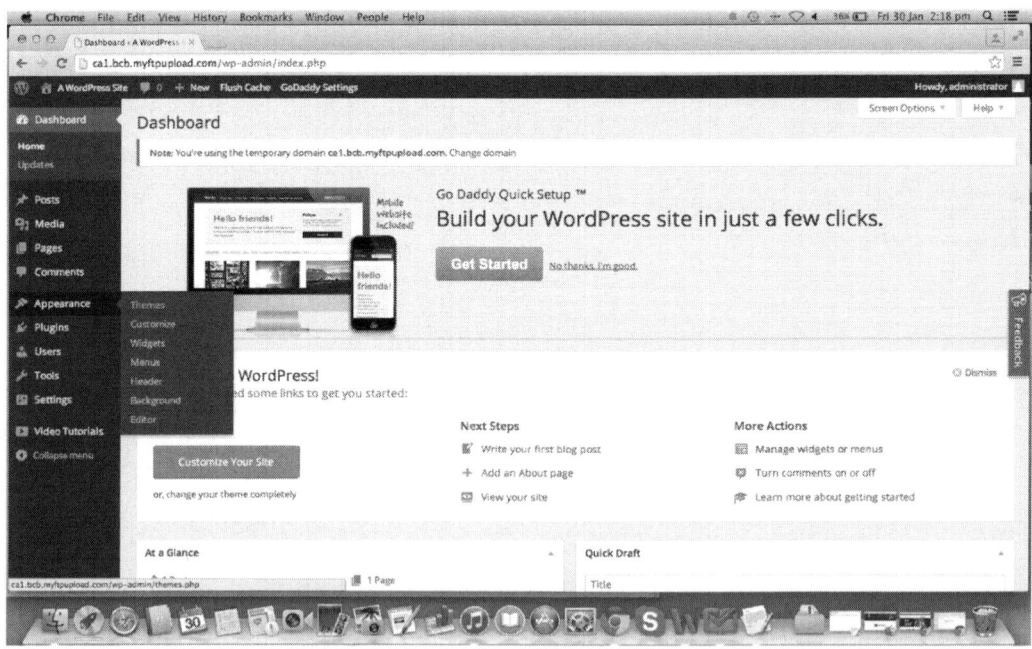

It's a piece of what makes Wordpress so effective. It is possible to alter the whole look of your site while never showing signs of change in the backend structure or content. Changing the theme is just a matter of a few clicks. So, technically, you are just a few clicks away from a completely revamped website. It can allow you to keep things current and updated using a much faster and more straightforward methodology. Subjects come in numerous sorts and mixed bags, including free and premium topics. You can likewise modify a topic to make it your own.

How To Install A Theme

Changing a theme is rather straightforward in wordpress. You just need to go to Appearance -> Themes. Once you have located this link on the dashboard, you are almost sorted. A click on this link will take you to the 'manage themes' page. It shall inevitably have a list of the themes that are installed on your wordpress account. You can activate any on of these themes if you feel that they can solve your purpose.

Most of the available themes have alternatives, including options and settings, which are open to changes. For example, gadgets, menus and other choices can be easily altered. These menus are accessible under Appearance, furthermore recorded under your current subject. These choices differ relying upon the topic, yet they may permit you to change the sidebar, change colors, and so on.

Remember that the objective is to change the theme. So, you initially need to introduce your theme to your wordpress account by installing it on the same. This will allow it to appear on your rundown of accessible themes in your themes section. Any theme will not be available in this section unless it is installed on your wordpress account. When a topic is there, you should simply click on 'Activate'. There are a few approaches that you can follow for installing new themes to your rundown of accessible themes:

Find and Install

Much like adding plugins, you can hunt down a subject and introduce it straightforwardly from Wordpress.org. If your theme of choice is listed in the rundown of themes available to you in the search result, you just need to install the same and it will appear in the list of available themes in your account. You can seek the Free Theme Directory right from wordpress. Discover a topic, you like. For this purpose, you can utilize the pursuit box or the gimmick channel to sort out the different alternatives.

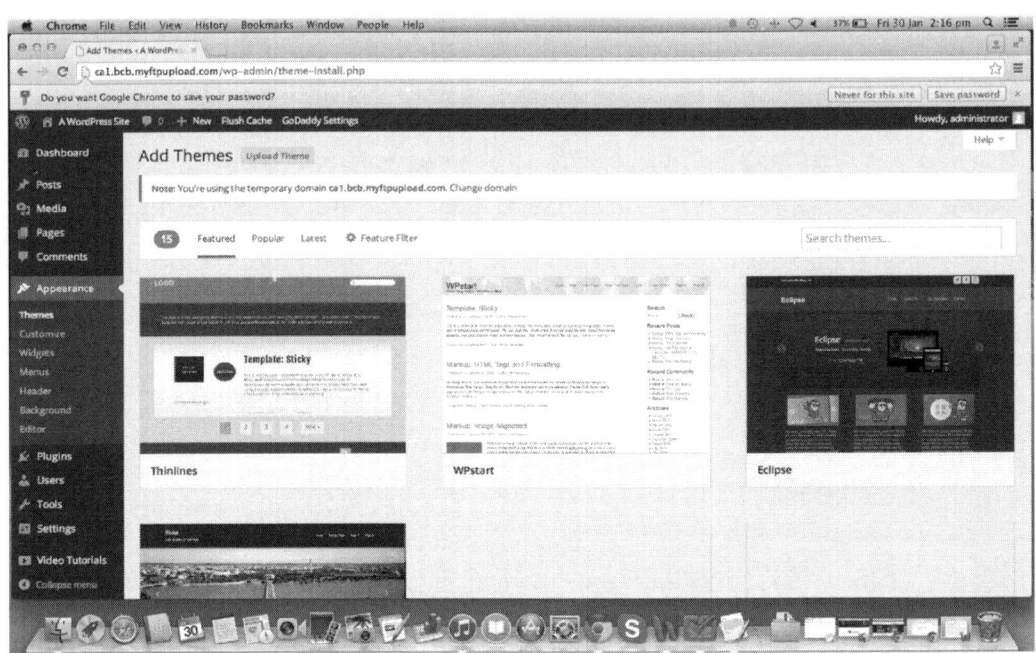

When you're taking a gander at a particular theme, you have a preview facility available to you to help you take a better look at the theme and the functionality it offers. It allows you to see a working website on the theme to help you make a better decision about whether you must install it or not. A few things may be choices you can modify yet different changes will oblige altering the code of wordpress files. When you discover a topic you like, click "Install." Once the subject is introduced, simply click "Activate." And much the same as that, your site has just took the ribbon off a new and refreshing look.

Download and Upload

The second choice is to download a topic from an outside source. This is the way by which most premium themes will need to be installed and introduced to your website. They generally come as a compressed document. At the highest point of the Install Theme page click on "Download" and you can transfer that file to your computer. Once it is transferred, you need to upload this file to the 'Add

Themes' section. Once it is completely uploaded, you need to install the same and activate it to complete the installation process.

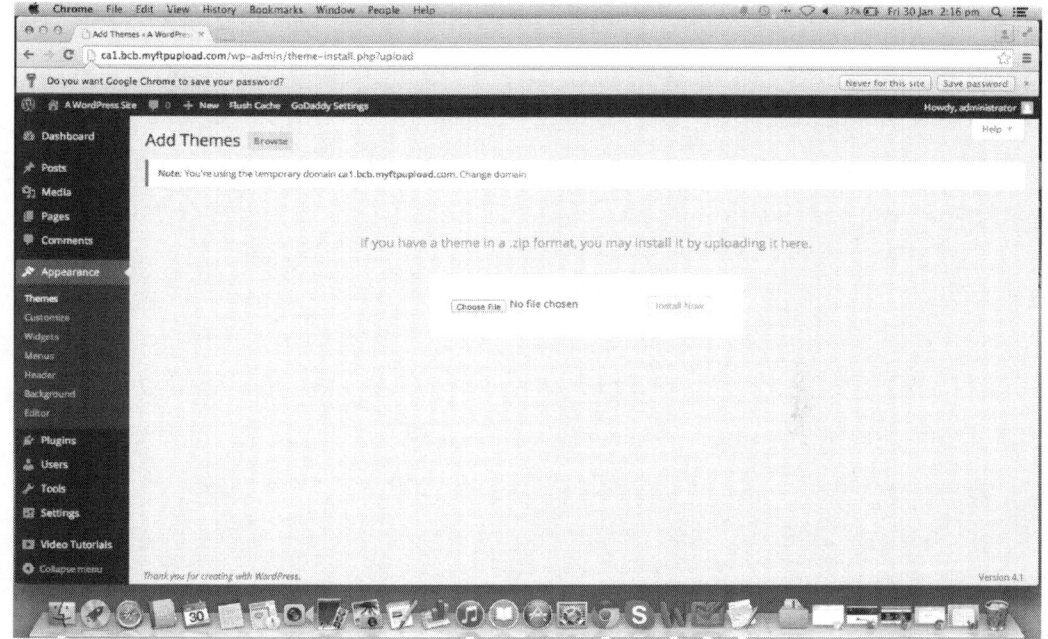

Manual Installation

You can likewise install themes by physically transferring them to your server. This can most effectively be performed using FTP. This is more entangled and not for the fledgling client. You'll have to download a topic to your machine and unzip it. This will provide for you an envelope on your machine with all the subject records. At that point, utilizing a FTP project, transfer the package. This package must be uploaded to the following location:

wp-content/themes

Once you have received an acknowledgement that the upload has been successfully done and installed, you can look for this theme in the list of installed themes on your wordpress account. All that you need to do here is to activate the theme and you are good to go.

Free Themes

The free themes directory of wordpress contains more than 1500 themes on different subjects and types of business/personal uses. This is an extraordinary spot to begin your quest for another subject. If you are truly clueless about the theme that will be the best for you, just mention the niche area to which your website belongs like business, photography, designing or writing, and you are sure to get awesome suggestions on which theme will be the best for you.

However, much the same as free plugins, once in a while you get what you pay for. Not all themes are made equivalent and with free topics you are more prone to discover places where developers and engineers took alternate ways. This isn't to imply that you shouldn't utilize a free option. Simply be mindful of what you're getting. Furthermore, be grateful. Somebody put a considerable measure of work into that topic and they're merciful doling it out for no charge. So, provide appropriate acknowledgement to the creator.

Premium Themes

Like we mentioned in the previous chapter, themes are also of two types: free and premium. The only difference between these two forms of plugins is that you need to pay a charge or get a license for using premium themes. At times, you pay for the topic itself, off and on again you pay a participation expense to get access to various subjects, and some of the time you're paying for backing to help you tweak the theme concerned. Wordpress has a rundown of premium subject suppliers. You may ask here as to why you should go for a paid theme if you have a free theme available to you.

Just as for anything that comes at a charge, premium themes offer much more to you than their free counterparts. They're more powerful, more proficient, have more choices and more noteworthy customization. Numerous premium subjects likewise have help accessible to help you make changes, such as changing colors or altering the sidebar. Contingent upon your ability level and what you require, it may be beneficial to pay somewhat additional and have help when you require it. No one but you can choose what the best fit is for you and your site.

Custom Themes

A theme alternative is to contract a developer or engineer for designing and developing a theme just for you. If you have preset requirements and none of the free or premium themes available seem to befit your idea, then going for custom development and designing is the only alternative left with you. There are a lot of designers out there making custom topics. Madebywheat.com is one custom-designing alternative we suggest.

Looking For A Theme

You cannot think of getting a theme that will be useful to you in any regard unless you know what you are looking for. It decides the look of your website and how the different elements will be laid out and how it functions. Furthermore, considering the large number of themes available in the Wordpress Directory and significantly more you can discover somewhere else, there's a considerable measure to look over. It's an enormous choice and you ought to put sooner or later into it. Before you plunge into those 1,500 topics like a child in a treat store, you ought to take a seat and give a good thought on what you need.

Assess your capabilities and limitations well in advance. Do you feel you can take a look into to CSS files to make alterations? Then again do you require a theme with a style director that gives you a chance to change the look without knowing code? Assuming this is the case, you'll presumably require a premium theme. Do you require exact levels of customization? Precise shades, specifically and tightly positioned sidebars and each component tightly located at the place that you want? Then again would you say you are eager to simply run with it? If you are looking for an option that does not require you to put any of your brains and efforts into coding and customization, you can conveniently go for the free theme option.

On the off chance that coding isn't your thing, yet you are critical, then a premium subject may be your call to make it simple to change things to your enjoying. You may also choose to hire someone to do the tweaking for you. Several contractual developers and freelancers can be contacted for this purpose. However, regardless of the choice you pick, be sure of what you want before starting. This will help you save both your time and money.

Some Tips For You To Consider While Choosing A Theme

- As you're perusing through topics, remember your confinements. On the off chance that you've chosen you would prefer not to disturb the code, look for a topic with a style director for simple customization or search for a subject that is precisely how you need it so it won't require any tweaking.
- What sort of site would you say you are making? If you are not creating a standard web journal, you may need to enlarge your hunt. Most free topics are centered on the straightforward website outline.
- Colors and header pictures are frequently alterable, so you should not stress over those. The most important thing here is to see if the structure of the theme suits you or not. Do you need one sidebar or two? Do you feel you need to change the menu's location? In case, you're ready to make changes, anything can be changed, however you need to discover a topic that needs the slightest customization.
- Browse through a subject's test site or sneak peek. Don't simply take a gander at the picture or a screenshot alone. Click on preview and navigate around the website to take an experience of how the user will perceive your website if you choose this theme. Explore through the site. Notice the contrasts between the landing page and the individual posts.
- Pay thoughtfulness regarding how a topic handles distinctive components. Do you like how block quotes and pictures are shown? Are pages and posts taken care of in an unexpected way?
- You may even need to download a topic and examine the code. Is it true that it is decently composed and simple to alter? There's nothing more

terrible than picking a topic and finding that the code is in frightful wreckage when you attempt to redo it.

- Make beyond any doubt your subject is good for the most recent rendition of wordpress. You need to exploit all the most up to date peculiarities and you can't do that with an antiquated topic. The additional time you spend on deciding what you need and after that selecting the right topic, the less baffled you'll be. You can simply change subjects effortlessly, yet you need to invest your time making substance, not always playing around with the design.

CREATING AND MANAGING MENUS

Wordpress makes menus simple. As you make new pages, you will feel the need to arrange them and organize them in such a manner that your users find it easy to navigate and look around your website. You can likewise add numerous layers of progressive system to your menu, include links to outside destinations and modify the request of your menu.

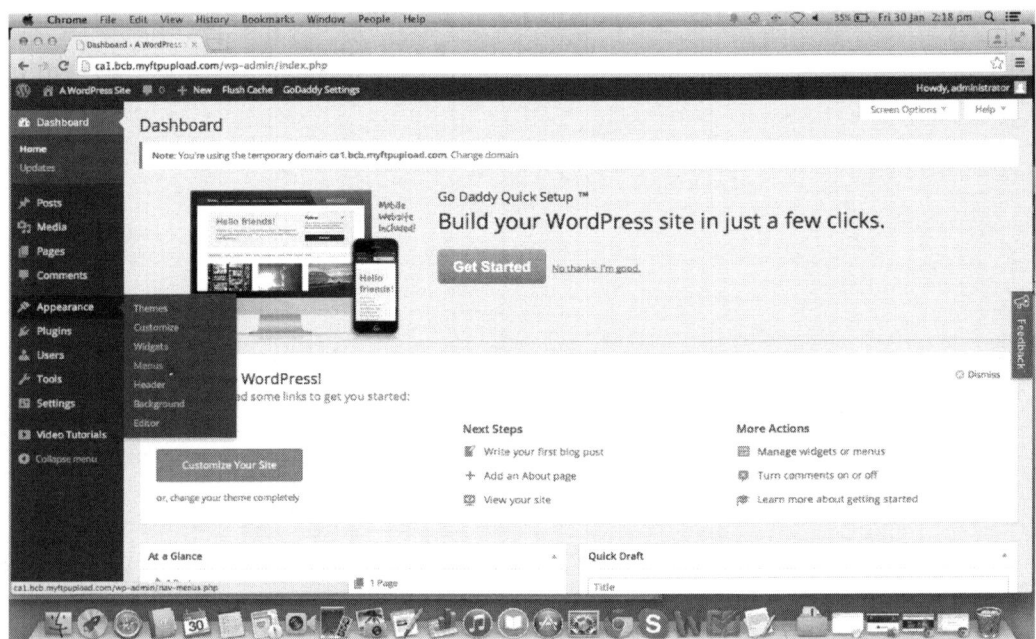

All these menu gimmicks make it simple for clients to explore your site and discover what they're searching for. Yet it likewise makes it simple to organize webpages on the website and simple to explore without the need for you to know how to code in wordpress. Also, you will not have to add every webpage you create the menu manually. Wordpress will automatically do that for you.

Out-of-the-Box Menu Functionality

Naturally wordpress offers a straightforward menu with a drop down route. That implies that when you move over a menu thing; drop down for alternatives will show up beneath. Setting up menus is extremely easy in wordpress and you just need to customize the given framework to create menus of your own. However, if you need a complete customization of your menus, you will need a little more knowledge of how to tweak into wordpress code.

Altering Your Menu

In case you wish to create a completely new menu for your website, for which you can control all the elements involved, you can do the same by adding a menu to the list of menus. You have the freedom to add the pages, links or any other elements that you wish to add to this menu. Whenever you wish to use this menu in your website, you can mention the menu name and wordpress will do the rest for you. You need to go to Appearance -> Menu to make your own menu. Initially, you have to make a menu and provide for it a name.

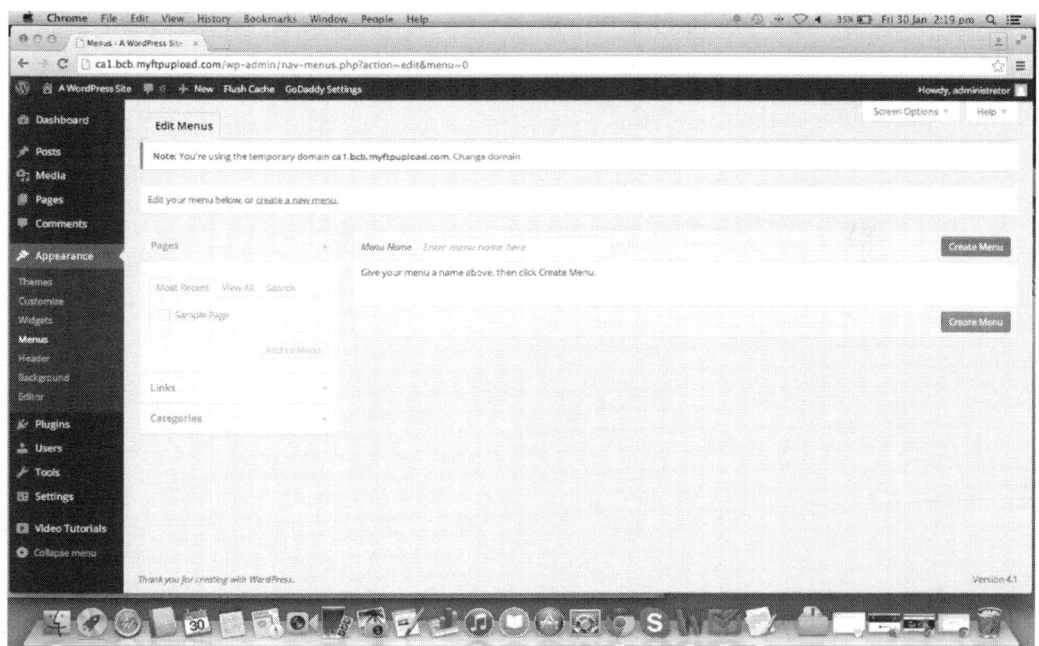

When you've made your menu, you can add things to it. You can choose from Custom Links, Pages and Categories. You can also click on "Screen Options" in the upper right corner to see a couple of more choices that are covered up naturally including Posts and Tags. If you wish to add pages to the menu you have created or an already existing menu, you need to check the containers beside the pages you need to show up in your route bar and click "Add to Menu".

Once you have added a few links to your menu, you have the liberty to move them around and change their order in the manner that you need. This reordering can also be performed for pages. You can likewise check the container to "Consequently include new top-level pages," however recall that in case you're demanding about the request you'll have to return and relocate them to the location where you wish them to appear on your page.

Once you're carried out making your menu, you can make it your primary menu by making a selection from the dropdown in Theme locations. To know more about how you can make changes to these, you can refer to the wordpress manual or user guide for the simple reason that creating custom menus may need specialized expertise and dedicated knowledge.

Overall, the functionality provided by wordpress, whether customized or default meets expectations incredibly, however it is exceedingly reliant on your subject. The default wordpress subject uses it and more current and expert themes will likewise exploit it. Yet in the event that you're utilizing a free theme, make beyond any doubt it exploits the latest menu options and functionality.

SEARCH ENGINE OPTIMIZATION

You need individuals to discover your site, so you have to verify it can be found. A real approach to do that is to focus on what is called Search Engine Optimization or SEO. The simplest definition o SEO is that it is a procedure to optimize your content in such a manner that web crawlers can easily rank your webpages. Moreover, you can work around with SEO to ensure that you get a good ranking in search results as well. Appearing higher in list items implies more individuals discovering your site.

There are some basic procedures that can help your SEO. Basically making content unique and relevant is an essential first step. The rule is simple. If you have more content, web crawlers have more content to list and you will be ranked higher. That is more ways a client can discover your site. It additionally implies you have more content for individuals to connect to. More connections from different destinations will likewise help your SEO.

Utilizing wordpress is a decent alternate approach to enhance your SEO. Wordpress is intended to be an inviting approach for creating your own website. Therefore, it is recommended that you start thinking on the SEO lines from the very beginning of the project. You can likewise utilize plugins to further support your SEO plan.

Some of the basic things that you must do to keep your content aligned with SEO and web crawlers is making updates regularly on your website. Moreover, the content that you add must be unique and relevant as far as a topic or subject is concerned. Secondly, be sure to make the use of permalinks. Permalinks are the best way to ensure that your website gets good visibility to search engines.

There are several plugins available in the wordpress community that can help you plan and implement your SEO effectively. One of the first steps that you need to take in this direction is to find the most appropriate plugin for this purpose. You may find paid as well as free variants. Some of the free to use plugins for SEO are All in One SEO pack and Yoast SEO.

All in One SEO Pack

This influential plugin is the most downloaded plugin in the Wordpress.org store. It is an extremely successful plugin that will help enhance your site's SEO. There are heaps of gimmicks you can use yet it has been found to be excessively useful for beginners and individuals who are willing to learn. There is a free form from the Wordpress.org storehouse, however you can likewise buy the ace form that incorporates help and drops the promotions, which are perfect for designers – or any individual who needs the certification of expert backing.

Yoast SEO

This is another free plugin that is available for you to use. It is an easy plugin to use if you are a beginner with Wordpress and SEO. The suggestions and instructions given for implementing SEO using this plugin are straightforward and easy to understand. Moreover, the plugin helps you with SEO gimmicks from the basic permalinks and header content of the advanced keyword density and content relevance. It is certainly a must try as and when you feel ready to go ahead with the SEO plan for your website.

USER COMMENTS – POLICIES AND SETTINGS

A most prominent aspect regarding web journals is the capacity to let users and readers remark or comment on your blog posts. This is also one of the most troublesome facets of web journals because unless you place a stern vigilance, you may not be able to control spammers or unwanted users from commenting on your blog.

Running a site with an open platform for commenting can be greatly remunerating and, now and again, baffling. Giving your users a platform to voice their assessment as this can help you refine your work, help you find new viewpoints and even provide for you a quite required congratulatory gesture. However, giving your users that opportunity can likewise open you up to a universe of migraines, spam and unlimited contentions.

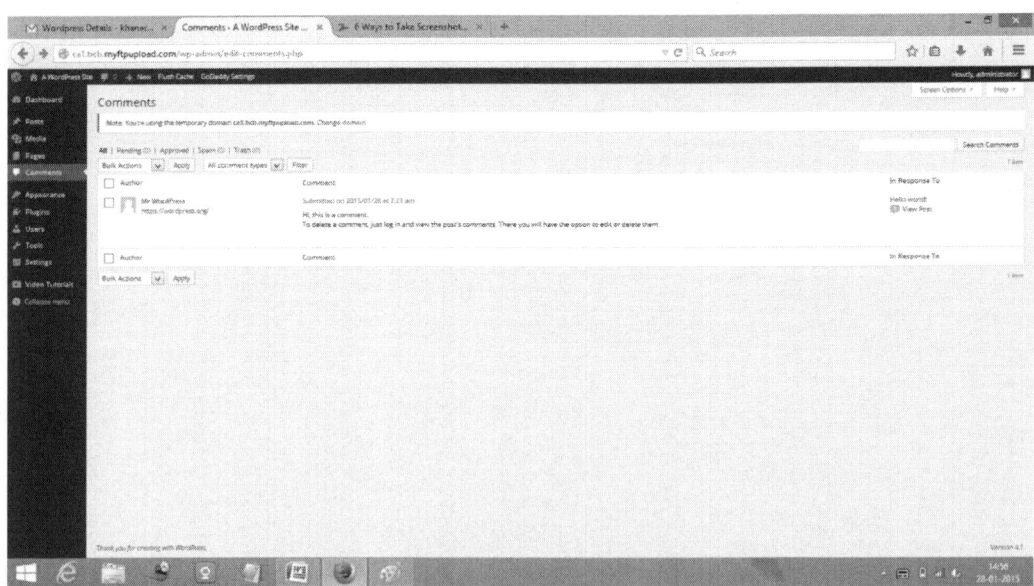

Be that as it may most bloggers will let you know the disadvantages, comments are worth the trouble at last:

- By giving your users a voice, you're demonstrating to them that they are so profitable to you. That sort of reliability means a great deal.

- Let's face it! You don't know everything as no one does. Allowing your users to comment is an unpretentious approach to concede that you're not flawless and permit your users to bail you out. In this manner, you will be able to make your website better. Moreover, it will also get you in a better position against your competitors.
- Often commitments of remarks will exceed the estimation of the first post. Frequently incredible thoughts will be imparted, linkages offered or monstrous talks that go on to become personal discussions, which mostly may not even be related to the topic of the post. Also, it is all on your site.
- It can fabricate groups. At the point, when individuals have a "voice" on your site, they feel esteemed and that what they say has any kind of effect. At last, whether to have remarks is a critical decision and one you shouldn't take daintily. You have to measure the upsides and downsides. You have to choose if open remarks fit your organization's style. For a few associations it is an impeccable fit. For others, it is ungainly.

In case, you're undecided about what to do with comments, you have some advice here to bail you out of this. There are a ton of midway arrangements. You're likewise welcome to alter your opinion and turn commenting on or off without restraint. Be that as it may, whatever you choose, it is best to pick an answer and stick to it. Your users will get confounded if commenting policy of your website is conflicting.

Policy for Commenting

When you've chosen to have comments, it is critical to have a strategy set up. It doesn't fundamentally must be open, yet you should seriously mull over it. What's imperative is to know how you're going to react in a particular circumstance and authorize your standards reliably.

- Are commentators permitted to utilize irreverence? What is the limit of non-sense that you are willing to take?
- It's simple for a comment string to get off subject. Are you fine with it or

are you just willing to take comments on the topic and discussion?

- Discussions frequently transform into verbal confrontations, which transform into level out contentions. Do you venture into restore request? Alternately let individuals duke it out?

- What do you do when somebody can't help contradicting you or your organization? Imagine a scenario in which that implies they suggest contenders.

- What happens when somebody disregards your tenets? You can very well escape these issues. In any case, it serves to be arranged. Regularly the style of your association will help you focus your comment policy and arrangement. A detached, happy go lucky association may urge individuals to oppose this idea. A strict, top-down organization may boycott any exchange of contending items.

Since the website is yours, the call is also yours. That is something else you'll have to choose. How dynamic would you as far as commenting is concerned on your part? Some individuals like to be extremely dynamic, empowering reactions and communicating with users. That can likewise be demanding, yet might likewise profit your business. Other individuals might just venture in when it is totally vital, letting their users have their own talk.

Settings For Comments

There are different varieties of settings accessible under Settings -> Discussions.

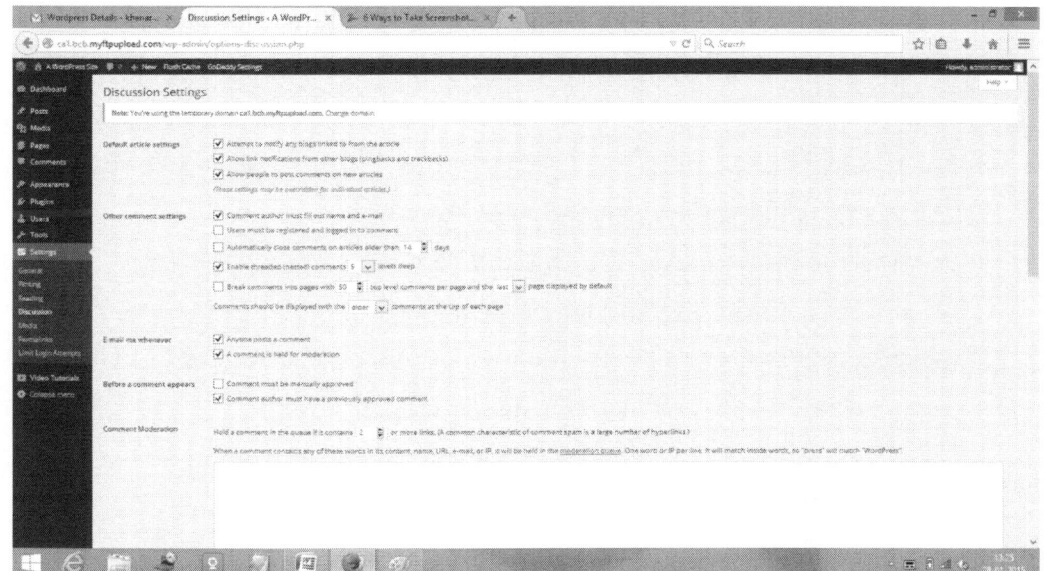

A significant number of them help to discourage remark spam.

- Default Settings – These settings are the default values that you will work with yet you can reset them to the values you want as far as individual posts are concerned. 'Permit individuals to post remarks on new articles' is the common one and this setting turns commenting on or off naturally.

- Other Comment Settings – These settings control how comments show up and how unknown clients can be.

- Email – You need to set these settings to tell wordpress to keep you advised of when, from whom and what comment your post has received.

- Comment Moderation & Comment Blacklist – You can filter comments automatically before publishing using these two methods. You can direct or totally square remarks for substance, name, URL, email or IP address. That implies you can include bothersome commentator' name or words you would prefer not to show up in your remarks These usually include obscenity, rival items, conceivably hostile subjects, and so on. It is not advisable, but it is a decent beginning.

- Avatars – Commenters can show a symbol alongside their remarks, including somewhat more identity. There are a few controls here. One of these is the default symbol for clients without pictures and picture content rating.

- Akismet
  Spam remarks can be a torment. These are futile remarks that normally incorporate a link to a spammer's site. Now and again spammers can be extremely unpretentious and you don't understand that they're spam. Akismet is a plugin, which can be searched for in the plugins section of Wordpress that can bail you channel out spam. You'll need to verify the plugin is introduced, actuated and in use for your website.

How To Manage Comments

You can favor, erase and deal with your remarks under the Comments section, which can be located in the left menu. This showcase will demonstrate all your current remarks. Over the top, you can get to file folders for particular sorts of remarks:

- Pending – Comments that are being held for balance. Therefore, these comments are awaiting your actions and cannot be seen by your users as yet.
- Approved – Your live remarks. These are the remarks that are right now available and can be seen on your site.
- Spam – Comments that have been stamped as spam.
- Trash – Comments that have been stamped as garbage and prepared to erase.

If you click the title of the comment concerned, you will be able to see the settings associated with that comment. You will additionally be able to make changes to the same.

- Approve/Unapproved – Removes a remark or posts.
- Reply – Allows you to answer to a remark inside Wordpress.

- Quick Edit – Allows you to rapidly alter the remark without expanding its full settings. This setting allows you to make only a few changes.
- Edit – Enters the full alter mode. This alteration can be done for each comment individually
- Spam – Marks the remark as spam.
- Trash – Moves the remark to junk. You can likewise get to the 'Mass Actions' dropdown at the base and utilize the checkboxes for each one remark to do different things immediately. So, if spam comments are your concern and you believe too many of them are hitting your website, you can check every one of them as spam and take the necessary action to relocate them to another folder marked as spam folder. Using the bulk action will make it easier and quicker for you to get rid of your spam.

Wordpress permits you to make users with particular permissions and rights. Distinctive aspects of user registration and control have diverse obligations and powers inside wordpress. This is critical on the off chance that you have a group of people taking a shot at your site. It permits you to follow a procedure where just a few authorized user can perform particular assignments, for example, publish posts. It's a decent approach to guarantee quality control, spread out obligation and hold everything under wraps. The users can be managed in the Users section of the dashboard, which has been discussed in greater detail in the following section.

USER MANAGEMENT

It is imperative that you are going to have users for your website. However, there shall be different types of users who will access your website. For instance, you or anybody from your team who visits the website for the sake of management and maintenance is not the general website user. It is necessary to make this distinction because each type of users shall have different rights on your website. While administrator or contributors have the right to post content, readers shall only have the right to comment.

In this chapter, you will see a rundown of clients and some fundamental data, including their part and what number of posts they've composed. Parts are critical owing to the fact that they decide how much access and control a client has over your wordpress website. There are five types of jobs as far as a wordpress website is concerned. These jobs are done by the following roles –

- Administrator –

  The admin has access to all managerial tasks. When you introduce and set up wordpress, you're naturally given an admin account.

- Editor –

  The editor can compose, alter and distribute posts and pages, and oversee other clients' posts.

- Author –

  The author can compose and alter their own posts, and distribute them.

- Contributor –

  The contributor can compose and alter their own posts, however they can't distribute them.

- Subscriber –

  The subscriber just needs to deal with his or her own profile. This part is more often than not for users or readers of your blog.

You'll have to thoroughly consider who ought to have what power, as this can be particularly crucial for you in the long run.

How To Add A User

You can make another user by going to Users -> Add New. Here you can enter the essential data to add a new user to the list. A username, email and watchword are the main fields that are needed. The greater part of the fields can be altered later, except for the username. Give careful consideration to this on the grounds that wordpress doesn't give you any cautioning: Once you make a user, you can never change their username. The username is the thing that they'll use to log into wordpress.

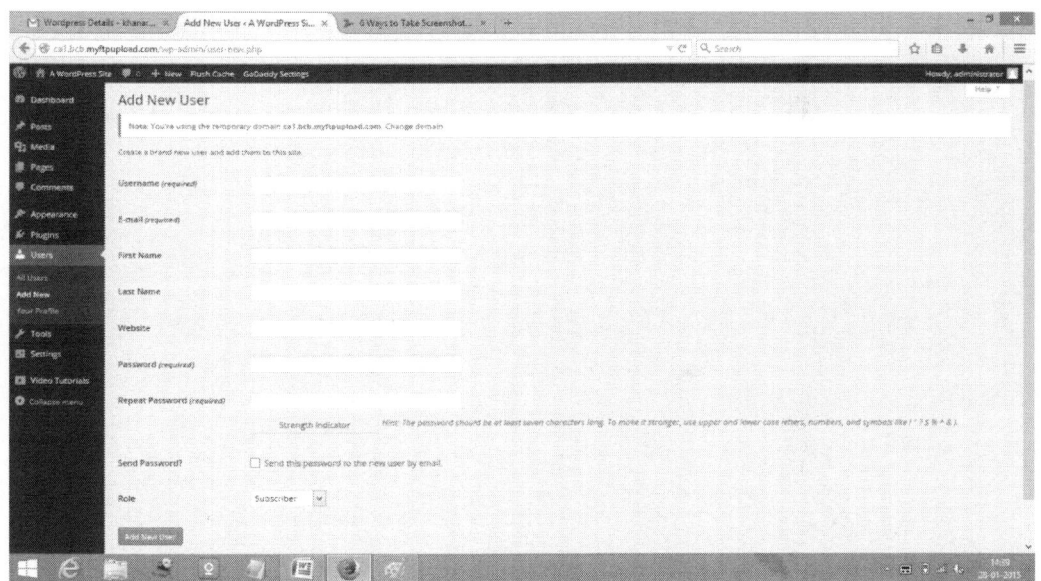

You can likewise permit users to list to your site. Under Settings -> General, there's an enrollment setting to allow anybody to enroll on your site. Contingent upon your theme, this will include a registration interface in the sidebar. There's additionally a dropdown there to choose the default setting for these new website users. Unless you need to give outsiders the ability to make or publish posts, you presumably need to leave the default on "Subscribers." Permitting individuals to enroll can be useful in the event that you need to support interaction or if you plan to give commenting rights only to enlist users alone.

How To Edit A User

If you have a created user, it will not be difficult to locate his or her name in the users list. You just need to click on the username of the concerned user and edit the details using the edit link given. Click on this link to get to the Profile alter screen.

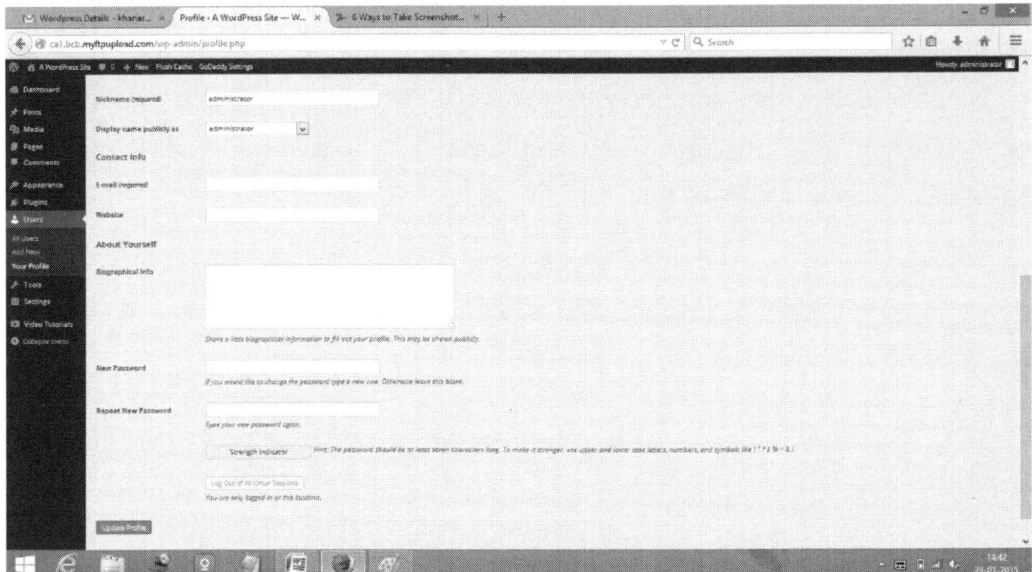

There are various useful alternatives here, most clear as crystal, however a couple could utilize some clarification:

- Visual Editor – If you need individuals to work with HTML content instead of visual content, you can compel them to utilize HTML by impairing the visual editor completing and give them access to only the HTML editor.
- Username – Note that the username can't be changed.
- Display name – the dropdown shall present to you several choices once you provide your name and email address details. This decides how Wordpress will show this current user's name.
- Biographical Info – This bio section can be alternatively shown. However, how this information will be shown totally depends on the theme you are using.

This can help you rapidly and effectively make creator pages for your website group. A quick tip for you here is that you must refrain from creating a user called 'administrator'.   Moreover, never set the password value as 'password'. These are the most commonly used values and your site can be at potential risk of attack and intrusion, in such a case.

COMMON WORDPRESS ERRORS

In all probability, if you are a wordpress user who likes to play around with the codes, or one who simply cherishes introducing modules and evolving themes, you will comprehend that experiencing a lapse is an unavoidable event. Wordpress users and developers know that it is so baffling to stagger into a surprising slip and not have the capacity to discover an answer for it. Most wordpress issues are feasible.

If you come across an error, don't fuss over it. Some Wordpress users and developers had the same issue and had as of now gotten it comprehended. In this chapter, we examine the absolute most basic five wordpress slips users have experienced, and offer with you the answers for fixing those issues or make them go away. We trust this will proves to be useful for you.

Admin Password and Email Retrieval Not Working

You lost your Wordpress administrator password, and have attempted to provide your username, ID or email address in the "Lost password?" page yet neglected to get any connection to make another secret key by means of email. Here are 2 straightforward answers for resetting your Wordpress password.

The first method makes use of phpmyadmin for this purpose. For using this method, you need to follow the below-mentioned steps –

- Login to the cpanel and click on phpmyadmin under Databases.
- Select your Wordpress database corresponding to users details.
- Go to wp_users and click on the browse data link.
- Look for your Username and click Edit.
- Reset the password in the table and remember the password that you have set. Also, remember that passwords are case-sensitive.

- Once you finished this, click the dropdown menu under Function, and pick Md5 from the menu and click go.

Dashboard Display Unavailable

The Wordpress administrator dashboard is showing without CSS. All the connections are not masterminded appropriately. Check if your Internet association is behind an intermediary association or firewall. Some of these devices are blocking CSS documents making CSS records to not stack appropriately. Attempt to clear your intermediary or firewall treats and store, and press Ctrl + F5 to revive your page. In the event that you have any Wordpress plugins introduced for the administrator menu, update it. On the off chance that it doesn't work, attempt to deactivate it.

Blank Page For Admin Page

This blunder typically happens directly after another Wordpress theme install or Wordpress update. The whole blog is demonstrating a clear page; so is the Wordpress administrator login page. There's no real way to get to the dashboard. Renaming the at present introduced topic envelope by means of FTP can compel Wordpress to pick the default theme to be put into administration and you're ready to get to Wordpress wp-administrator after that.

Error 403

You get a lapse message "You are not authorized to view this page. (Error: 403)" in the wake of embeddings the username and password in the Wordpress administrator login page. In the event that your online journal is facilitated on a Windows server, this could be a lapse in Directory Indexes. In order to fix this issue, you need to follow the following steps:

- Login to the Control Panel.
- Click on Web Options.
- Go to Directory Indexes segment.
- Add index.php to the Directory Indexes.

Unable To Delete A Plugin

You're not ready to erase a plugin in Wordpress administrator. Despite everything it seems much after you have erased the registry by means of FTP. Your plugin may have transferred some shrouded/settled records inside the plugin registry which didn't show up in FTP. On the off chance that you have SSH access to your web journal, you can do the following:

- Login your site through SSH.
- Navigate to the location "../wp-content/plugins/" using SSH commands.
- The list of folders can be found using ls -al command.
- Delete the specific plugin folder with rm.

Other Programming Books You Might Enjoy:

jQuery, JavaScript, and HTML5: A Simple Start to jQuery, JavaScript, and HTML5 (Written by a Software Engineer)

C++ Programming For Beginners: A Simple Start To C++ Programming Written By A Software Engineer

PHP Programming and MySQL For Beginners: A Simple Start To PHP & MySQL Written By A Software Engineer

Java For Beginners: A Simple Start To Java Programming

C Programming: The C Programming Language Guide For Beginners (Written By A Software Engineer)

HTML and CSS For Beginners: A Simple Start To HTML & CSS (Written By A Software Engineer)